STRATEGI
THE TIM]

The
Six Pillars
of
Productivity

Cindy B. Sullivan, CPO®

THE SIX PILLARS OF PRODUCTIVITY: Strategies to Organize the Time of Your Life
Copyright © 2023 by Cindy B. Sullivan, CPO®
Published by Station Square Media
115 East 23rd Street, 3rd Floor
New York, NY 10010
www.Stationsquaremedia.com

All rights reserved. No part of this book may be reproduced, stored in a retrieval system, or transmitted in any form or by any means, electronic, mechanical, or otherwise, without the prior written permission of the publisher, except for brief quotations in articles and reviews.

Editorial: Write to Sell Your Book, LLC
Cover and Interior Design: Steven Plummer, SP Design
Post-Production Management: Janet Spencer King

Printed in the United States of America for Worldwide Distribution

ISBNs: 979-8-9887620-2-7 (trade paperbook), 979-8-9887620-0-3 (hardcover), 979-8-9887620-1-0 (ebook)

First Edition
10 9 8 7 6 5 4 3 2 1

DEDICATION

This book is dedicated to those who have shared with me their challenges, questions, experiences, failings, successes, strengths, and dreams. Allowing me into your world so we could explore the gift of time and how to use it wisely was what planted the seeds of inspiration for this book. You've taught me so much and for that I am grateful.

TABLE OF CONTENTS

Part One: The 6 Pillars Evolution & Why this Approach is Different 7
   Why I Wrote This Book. 9
   Making This Book Work for You 13
   What Does It Mean to Be "Productive?" 17
   Introducing the 6 Pillars 23

Part Two: Putting the Pillars to Work for You 31
   Pillar 1: Planning 33
      Step 1: Create a Schedule Model. 40
      Step 2: Develop a Planning Routine. 50
      Step 3: Adapting When the Plan Changes 58
      Key Takeaways. 60
   Pillar 2: Internal Time Clock 63
      Step 1: Set Mile Markers 69
      Step 2: Make the Passage of Time "Relatable" 71
      Step 3: Utilize Time Tracking. 74
      Step 4: Reflect Back. 76
      Key Takeaways. 78
   Pillar 3: Long-Range Goals. 79
      Step 1: Set the Stage 86
      Step 2: Brainstorm. 90
      Step 3: Evaluate 93
      Step 4: Identify & Target 94
      Step 5: Make Goals "Actionable" 99
      Step 6: Anticipate the Hurdles 101
      Key Takeaways. 102

Pillar 4: Leverage: Habits & Behaviors 103
   Step 1: Listen for Internal Dialog 111
   Step 2: Build Habits for the Win 113
   Step 3: Work the Plan. 117
   Step 4: Get Going!. 121
   Step 5: Stop what's Stopping you 129
   Step 6: Optimize your Work with Others. 142
   Key Takeaways. 151

Pillar 5: Arrangement 153
   Step 1: Identify and Address "Clutter". 160
   Step 2: Sort and Categorize 165
   Step 3: Plan Your Space with Purpose. .168
   Step 4: Designate a Space for Everything 171
   Step 5: Maintain it All 176
   Online & Digital Organization. 178
   Key Takeaways. 184

Pillar 6: Resources 187
   Step 1: Consider your Calendar 193
   Step 2: Capture and Manage your Tasks. 195
   Step 3: Select the Right Planning Tools for YOU. 200
   Key Takeaways. 207

Part Three: Appendix (Forms & Samples). 213
Weekly Calendar/Schedule Model Template. 214
Sample 1: Low structure/High Responsiveness role 215
Sample 2: High Structure/Low Responsiveness role 216
Sample 3: Blend of low and high structure days 217
Weekly Planning Page Template. 218
Time Log Samples 219

PART ONE

THE 6 PILLARS EVOLUTION & WHY THIS APPROACH IS DIFFERENT

WHY I WROTE THIS BOOK

FRUSTRATION. OVERWHELM. STRESS. Guilt. These are just a few of the emotions shared with me by clients over the years. They recognize that their time is a resource for accomplishing what is important to them but don't feel they are using it wisely. I've heard from people who voice their dreams but feel stuck in moving them closer to reality. Some have missed opportunities while their attention was distracted by other urgencies. Still, others have felt they are "spinning their wheels"—never gaining traction or making headway. These individuals are motivated, smart, and successful. They include entrepreneurs, homeschooling parents, managers, students, physicians, and more. What they have in common is their desire to experience a higher level of productivity and satisfaction. They want a strategy to improve how they operate.

The willingness of these individuals to share their experiences and explore with me what is behind their struggles helped me craft the approach I now share with you. You are the beneficiary of that exploration. I invite you to begin this journey by first expanding your thinking around *TIME*. Perhaps you've experienced some of the same challenges listed above. Maybe you aim to sharpen your skills to work smarter. The 6 Pillars provide a better understanding of where to begin so that you feel more fulfilled, quit wasting time, and boost your productivity. You can find answers and formulate a targeted approach to start seeing change!

Productivity isn't a destination, just as health isn't a destination.

There is no finish line where once you reach it, the work is done. It is active. It requires attention. And it's not only about finding the right tools or method to put in place *once*. I aim to help you team your personal style with techniques and tools that best manage your focus and actions, both today and as circumstances change: This combination can help you accomplish the things you want and need to get done.

There is no single path that all individuals are on as they move to increase their productivity.

As clients welcomed me into their worlds, we'd begin to uncover their stumbling blocks and inefficiencies. What was a struggle for one person was a strength for another. Having these widely varied conversations with each individual client highlighted that productivity challenges span multiple distinct areas. It also became clear that those areas are intertwined. Exploring these "Pillars" with clients helped paint a clearer picture of how each person functioned in all the different areas that impact their use of time. The answer was rarely as simple as how to make a task list, avoid distractions, and find ways to save time. The results have been amazing, and I want to share with you the value of understanding and incorporating the 6 Pillars into your own productivity journey.

The Pillars make Productivity and Time Management less obscure and easier to visualize and understand.

Clients tell me they finally "get it!" The Pillars make sense. Breaking down productivity into distinct areas allows us to address more concrete topics, drawing a clear line between the skills we are sharpening and where its impact is seen. Rather than sampling a wide array of time-saving tips and techniques, focus can be given to those needing attention, and—bonus—recognition goes to things functioning well.

Lastly, Productivity isn't always about packing *more* into your days.

It's about being more efficient with the *have to*'s so you have more time for the *want to*'s. It's the satisfaction that comes when your days include activities you find rewarding, meaningful, and even fun. And I haven't met anyone who doesn't want more time for that!

MAKING THIS BOOK WORK FOR YOU

Where to begin

EACH OF US learns differently, and I've worked to provide a book that allows flexibility in its use with resources aimed at helping you customize and retain its content. First, I'd like to address how you can navigate the coming chapters. While each of the 6 Pillars has its own dedicated section and can be reviewed independently, I recommend all readers first progress through the upcoming sections beginning with "What it Means to be Productive" through the first Pillar chapter before skipping to another area. These sections include foundational information on productivity and an overall review of the pillars that will help set the stage for the chapters ahead. Also, I consider the first Pillar (*Planning*) to be a central activity that can support your efforts in each of the other Pillars. At the completion of that chapter, you can proceed through the Pillars in the order they are written, or you may choose to target another Pillar next. I'll share a bit later the reasons that I recommend ultimately including ALL the Pillars in your review but know that the order you address them is up to you.

Key Takeaways & Self-Tests

You'll find a Key Takeaways section included at the end of each chapter which serves as a compilation of the info covered and provides a wrap-up and reminder when you revisit each Pillar. Plenty of questions and Self-Tests are also included throughout the book. These are valuable in helping you pinpoint and commit to those areas you want to highlight, acknowledge, and improve. Reading is one way to process information, but making targeted commitments and decisions takes it a step further toward holding yourself accountable for change.

Tips & Techniques

Every Pillar contains multiple tips & techniques for strengthening your skills in that area. My clients served as my best reminder through the years that what works for one person may not work for another. For that reason, I've offered up a variety of methods I've utilized with different clients. **Don't aim to employ every option or idea provided. Look for those that resonate with you and feel like the most natural approach.** Revisit that area if you wish to try other or additional techniques. You know YOU best.

The 6 Pillars Assessment

The 6 Pillars assessment, originally developed for use with my clients, is available online as an additional, free resource at www.6PillarsProductivity.com. This questionnaire spans all 6 areas and will return a score for each Pillar. The higher the score, the more you may wish to strengthen that area. You are welcome to take it before reading further to provide a baseline, after completing the book, or at different stages to gauge progress. **Know that the assessment is not required to understand or interpret this book.** You can review the information contained in these pages and find ways it relates to your world, with or without the assessment results. If scoring helps you track and make progress, use it. If it isn't helpful to you, forgo it. As with the many techniques in this book, take or adapt those resources that can help you, and set aside those you don't need or don't feel beneficial.

WHAT DOES IT MEAN TO BE "PRODUCTIVE?"

"I was busy ALL day yet got nothing meaningful done!"

SINCE THE GOAL is to help you identify and address those skills needed to uphold productivity, it's important to first understand what the word—*Productivity*—means to you. I've seen clients struggle with what they KNOW to be vital activities in their role, yet their instinct is to spend time elsewhere so they can FEEL productive in the moment. I've witnessed people go through a variety of life changes. Whether retiring, starting a family, making partner, changing careers, or moving into a new profession the change might mean that productivity looks different than before and feels foreign. That disconnect can impact where your attention, action, and focus are directed.

Textbook definitions for productivity bring up words such as "abundance," "yield," "richness," and "fertility." It considers the input and effort we invest compared to the output and results toward our intended purpose. **The measurement of whether an activity is**

productive lies in its outcome. Does the energy we invest yield the result we desire? Yet I often see people weigh their effectiveness solely on their actions or **input**—with the expectation that a large quantity of activity or "busyness" translates to productivity. We've all had those days when we feel that despite being busy all day, we accomplished nothing meaningful. It's frustrating when that high level of effort and input doesn't seem to align with our larger intentions or values. A struggle may be going on between **Checklist, Deep Focus,** and **Rabbit Hole Productivity.**

CHECKLIST PRODUCTIVITY

You experience Checklist Productivity when you do work that is specific and purposeful. These actions likely represent many of your day-to-day tasks, and they support your life, family, or work. Checklist activities can be put on your calendar or a to-do list and are well-defined with a beginning and an end.

Examples can be:

- Participating in meetings
- Processing reports
- Attending continuing education classes
- Running errands
- Sending/answering emails
- Organizing
- Logging your work expenses
- Taking the kids to gymnastics
- Tackling a work or home project

Checklist activities have the benefit of feeling good "in the moment" as you get them done and, in hindsight, since they support those things you want to accomplish. It's rewarding when you can check them off your list! Productivity here is tangible and recognizable.

DEEP FOCUS PRODUCTIVITY

Deep Focus Productivity feels much more ambiguous and provides less feeling of completion. These activities require brainwork and focus on a topic. Some examples are:

- Strategic planning
- Analysis
- Leadership activities
- Self-development
- Relationship-building
- Writing
- Evaluating the impact and results of an approach
- Meditation or prayer

While incredibly valuable, they are prone to being set aside. There is less definition about what exactly is to be done. You may not have a specific endpoint or due date and may not get the rush of endorphins that come with checklist activities. Intentional focus is required to sustain them, and it can be easy to put them on the back burner while reaching to address more tangible activities. The good news is that the payoff—the **output**—for these activities is usually high and very rewarding. By breaking them down into smaller steps (creating checklist activities), persevering, developing good habits, and recognizing the value of Deep Focus Productivity, you can become more comfortable holding space for work in this area.

RABBIT HOLE PRODUCTIVITY

Lastly, there is a third type of activity that is often disguised as productivity. Have you ever churned through emails without addressing any, gotten side-tracked while on the Internet, or had meandering phone calls or conversations? By capturing our attention and focus, we may *feel* productive in the moment, yet those activities don't yield much value and can end up a giant time suck! Rabbit Hole activities may even start as legit tasks. But, when done to an extreme (such as that "quick" RSVP email response that you end up spending 20-30 minutes to write, re-write, then ditch in favor of picking up the phone), they take up residence alongside timewasters. Let's see some other examples of what these might look like:

- Researching options ad nauseam for decision-making. (Information is practically unlimited on the internet, and too much time can be spent trying to gather ALL info rather than gathering ENOUGH to make a choice.)

- Unproductive meetings that are more routine than based on need

- Multi-tasking, where too many things get slivers of your attention yet not enough to get down to more deep and meaningful work

- Getting online for one purpose but falling prey to distractions and message notifications

- Games

- Overuse of social media

- Errands done at random times vs. planning them for efficiency and for more appropriate times

What Does It Mean to Be "Productive?"

We've all fallen prey to wasteful activities at times. We're human. Some serve as a mental break or even relaxation—think YouTube videos, social media, or games. Other times they help us avoid something we don't really want to address or are unsure how to begin. Putting energy here provides a balm to our emotions and distracts us when we feel overwhelmed. We're locked in and engaged, so time passes quickly. All those other pressing matters fade into the background. And since we're active and busy, it can *feel* like productivity . . . but it isn't. Going down a rabbit hole is deceptive, and it rarely leaves us feeling good about it once we are past the initial endorphins it provides.

As you work to build and strengthen your productivity skills, a good first step is identifying what productivity looks like in your world and recognizing which activities support that. What balance of Checklist and Deep Focus Productivity is beneficial to your role? Where are you susceptible to going down a Rabbit Hole?

Consider where you are NOW as well as where you want to be. Periodically revisit it. As you progress in your career and life, your needs change. The activities you are taking on today may not be relevant in two years. Likewise, new circumstances may warrant a different type of productivity altogether. So, before we move on to the 6 Pillars, I encourage you to set aside a block of time. Find a comfortable spot, grab your favorite beverage, and limit distractions. The self-test on the next page aims to help you define what productivity means for YOU. That self-knowledge is a vital building block for the strategies coming up in the following chapters.

PRODUCTIVITY
SELF-TEST

START WHERE YOU ARE RIGHT NOW.......

If you were to break down your role(s), what percentage of Checklist vs. Deep Focus Productivity is needed?

Where are you susceptible to Rabbit Hole Productivity disguised as Checklist or Deep Focus?

What activities are NOT productive for you? What can you change to alleviate or lessen time spent on them?

What other people, positions, etc., are impacted by your productivity?

When you are operating at optimal productivity—what does that look like?

INTRODUCING THE 6 PILLARS

SINCE STARTING MY career in the field of Productivity and Time Management, I've met with clients from all walks of life. Some exhibited strengths in planning yet struggled to stay on track. Others easily maintained focus throughout their day but felt like they were never able to accomplish all they should. Or they lacked motivation and energy to enact the bigger plans and goals they'd envisioned for themselves. As a Certified Professional Organizer®, I began work with some clients by first helping them address their physical environment. I saw how their struggles to work and live in their space made activities take longer or even fail to happen altogether. Things didn't add up the same way for every client. As I explored a challenge with one client, I'd see the value in adding that exploration with the next.

I started to expand my inquiries with individuals to fully understand what was impacting their productivity. It was from this series of questions that I saw the themes emerge that were to become the 6 Pillars and form the basis of my 6 Pillars Assessment. I've been affirmed in the years since its inception to see the 6 Pillars utilized with positive results for so many.

I chose the term "Pillar" for two reasons. First, a pillar's job is to bear weight and provide support. That is exactly what the 6 Pillars do! Picture a columned structure where the roof symbolizes your *Maximum Productivity*. Each Pillar helps lend support to hold up your effectiveness and comprises its own unique skills and knowledge. When a Pillar is weak, it isn't holding up its share of the load. That can be sustainable for a while, but it puts more pressure on the other Pillars to compensate for those that aren't strong. Add even more weight—through a growing workload, increased responsibility, busier schedules, etc., and maintaining what was once manageable can become unbearable. Cracks can appear, and things may begin to crumble or break down.

Secondly, the acronym P.I.L.L.A.R. itself highlights the key elements that I've found crucial to my client's productivity. These six areas encompass all the various skills and actions that help us operate at our best. Each provides unique support. They are:

- **Planning** - Creating a roadmap and structure for your time
- **Internal Time Clock** - Developing your time awareness
- **Long-Range Goals** - Identifying your "big picture" and how to get there
- **Leveraging your Habits & Behaviors** - Building skills for better focus and purpose
- **Arrangement** - Organizing your space for optimal efficiency
- **Resources** - Maximizing your use of tools that keep you on track

Planning

Planning incorporates how you make decisions and strategize which tasks and projects deserve your time in the coming days. Just as a roadmap charts a course toward a specific destination, **a plan keeps the end goal in mind. You select activities and target your focus so that priorities—not minutia—take precedence.** It serves as a reference tool throughout your week and reflects how you can best structure your time to get it all done.

How can you build a schedule that honors your work style and encompasses all the important categories? What does that day or week look like? Where do activities best fit? The purpose of the Planning Pillar is to identify *what* needs to be accomplished and *how* you can lay out a blueprint to make it happen.

Internal Time Clock

We often measure time by the minutes and hours on the clock, but we also experience time through our actions and activities. A strong Internal Time Clock reflects **your awareness of the passage of time in relation to your activities**. Some people are very intuitive about what time it is and how much time has elapsed. Others lose track of time easily. Also at play in this Pillar is knowledge of the quantity of time required to complete various tasks. Taking on a new role, new activities, or even habitually multi-tasking can make it hard to accurately gauge just how much time things will take to complete, which can throw off your ability to forecast and plan with accuracy.

Long-Range Goals

Incorporating a long-range view means extending the landscape beyond what's in front of you today to what is on the horizon. It boosts productivity and satisfaction when you expand your actions to reflect the goals you envision for your life. Consider not only what needs to be done today or tomorrow but also what can happen to further your bigger dreams and ambitions. Are you clear about where you want to head in your life or career? That can be defined as a specific achievement, a project, a lifestyle you wish to lead, or things you want to add or subtract from your life. This Pillar also covers the awareness of *how* to act on those intentions. This Pillar encompasses both **the capacity to identify your goals and what's most important to you as well as understanding the steps you must take to get there.**

Leveraging your Habits & Behaviors

This Pillar looks at the skills within you that support or hinder your effective use of time. **How well are you managing your focus and actions so that you can be your most productive self?** This Pillar is an umbrella that covers many strategies we all need to use frequently. Topics such as overcoming procrastination, delegation, handling interruptions, staying focused, effective communication, and establishing routines are included here. It pertains to self-management skills that help us be productive.

Arrangement

The layout and order within a space drive its functionality. Organizational techniques in this Pillar help you **create an area where you can find what you need when you need it.** Searching for items you need or recreating work affects our productivity, not to mention the distractions and stress it adds to our environment. Is your workspace, office, or home set up so you can easily access those things you need most frequently? Can you locate, access, and store digital files and information with confidence? Is storage set up in a way to allow easy retrieval of items when you need them? Is it as easy to put things away as it is to leave them out where they may get mislaid or lost? Is clutter at a minimum so you have fewer visual distractions—whether in the office, at home, or on your computer's desktop?

Resources

Professionals of all types recognize the benefit of having the best resources at their disposal and using them well. Tools and techniques that support your time use are just as important and greatly boost your effectiveness. Are you proficient with managing your calendar? Do you have a method to capture what needs to be done and when? Are there places where you need to establish workflows, implement a new process, or learn to use systems more efficiently? What types of prompts and reminders work for you? **These tools and skills keep you on track.**

This introduction is a very high-level look at the 6 Pillars. In the coming chapters, we'll be moving into a deeper exploration of each Pillar and demonstrating how they all support you in your day-to-day world. You'll discover how vulnerabilities in these areas impact your ability to operate at your best as well as learn which tips and techniques reinforce each Pillar. Additionally, I hope to shine a light on those areas where you have strengths but may not have considered how those strengths support your efforts to be productive. Many focus on their areas of difficulty, and even pain, vs. seeing where things already work well. We seek to fix first those things we see as "broken" rather than capitalizing on our strengths.

One last consideration I want to offer up before we proceed is to look across all six areas not only as independent and unique but reliant on one another. The earlier illustration of a pillar helping support the weight of others that are weak applies to these Pillars as well. There have been times when client work has led us to address one challenge only to find that the root problem existed in a different Pillar than we had first targeted.

Allow me to share two real-life examples here.

Solving a Productivity Puzzle

I first met David, a 45-year-old small business owner, when coaching one of his staff members. I was working with his employee to better structure her work activities and stay more organized. After one of my sessions, he pulled me aside and asked if I could work with him to solve a productivity puzzle of his own. David was an avid planner. He would regularly and diligently review all he needed to do and build a plan, yet he never seemed able to get everything accomplished. He asked if I could help. An initial discussion suggested that he needed to adapt his schedule, perhaps find a new planning system, or work to decrease distractions. As we began to look closer, he revealed he would get absorbed in tasks and spend too much time on activities, entirely losing track of his day. Not only did he miss the mark on planning an appropriate number of tasks or projects to try to conquer in a day, but he also had no idea just how long his morning routine took and couldn't accurately estimate the time it took for him to get into the office and begin his workday. We realized his Internal Time Clock was weak. To exclusively continue to revisit the areas of planning and changing his habits would have been to rely on those Pillars to take the weight vs. working to improve his time awareness so that it could support him.

A Case of "Should"

Margot came to me with a specific request to address her schedule and set up systems to keep her on track. A young, energetic professional, she had recently begun work at a new financial planning firm and had big goals that involved bringing in new business. A sticking point came up with a marketing campaign she stated was a top priority but in which she couldn't seem to make progress. We broke it down into very specific next steps and discussed hurdles that were getting in her way.

Things stalled, and the marketing plan still wasn't addressed. So, we worked to shift her schedule, allowing dedicated time to work on it. She stated that she now had everything she needed to begin—claiming it wouldn't take long and was straightforward. She sounded motivated and ready to jump into action when we completed our coaching session.

Still, the task continued to roll over from one week to the next. We then talked about different ways to approach the problem, and that is when she provided a vital clue: she wasn't that excited about this type of campaign, even questioning whether it would bring in the type of clients that were her best fit. It turns out that she wasn't engaged at all with this initiative. She felt she "should" be doing it. When I asked her, "If you could generate clients another way without ever having to do this type of marketing event, how would you feel?" Her answer? "Fantastic!"

Before taking a broader look, we were putting the focus on the wrong Pillar. We were bolstering up her planning and how she was structuring her time, but that wasn't where the problem was rooted. What she needed was to reconnect with her Long-Range Goals, her desire to bring in new business and change things up, and to find an alternative marketing initiative so she would be motivated rather than discouraged. Then, our work to structure her time and keep her on track could prove fruitful.

What might you find if you broaden your scope to include a look at all the Pillars? What impact is possible if you enhance each area with small, doable changes vs. homing in on one area only? What if you learned how to capitalize on your strengths to leverage what you already do well? There may be an answer to your own productivity mystery hiding where you least expect it! Are you ready to begin? Let's dive in now to explore the first Pillar. Because once time has passed, it can't be reclaimed.

PART TWO

PUTTING THE PILLARS TO WORK FOR YOU

PILLAR 1
PLANNING

WHEN YOU START your day, where do you begin? Do you have a clear picture of your priorities for the day and week, or do you need to cycle through email, post-its, or stacks to decide what needs your attention next? How do you make room in your schedule to work on bigger life goals? Perhaps you have a good place to capture and track everything you need or want to get done. That's great! But if you work from one massive list, it can be overwhelming and difficult to know where to start. Do you plan your week but find that urgencies take over? **We all benefit when we have a reference tool or road map that can help us navigate our days and aim us toward our bigger goals.** That's exactly what the Planning Pillar provides.

Planning is your opening move—your first step—toward being more productive. It is much more than list-making or doing a brain dump of everything necessary floating around your mind. **This Pillar is about being purposeful with when, where, and how you choose to direct your energy and attention.** We will factor in not only the tasks that need doing but the architecture of your days as well. How can you best lay out your activities to maximize when and how things get done? Do you struggle with the idea of living with *structure*? Some clients have said they feel like the walls are closing in when they hear that word! So let's shift from the mental image of a *structure* being a building or container that holds things inside to that of a bridge—a structure that facilitates crossing from one point to a new destination. It helps us get from Point A to Point B efficiently and purposefully. The structure supports the road that will take you where you want to go.

As you develop strength in this Pillar, you ensure that you're spending your time on the things that matter most. What are those things for you? When you look at all you are and do, what are the main themes that emerge? What balance of checklist and deep focus activities are needed in your days? Are there areas of responsibility or relationships that deserve more time and attention? What activities need a home in your schedule so that they stay on target? The work of Planning is like packing for vacation. You don't simply throw the first items you come across into a suitcase—**you first determine what you want and need to take and then how to make it all fit!**

When you plan, you step back from the day-to-day work to think strategically and make decisions. It is a time to look at the weeks ahead and make purposeful choices about the tasks that will prepare you for what's coming. It holds space for the activities you determine are most important—intentionally building them into your schedule. It's so very easy to get caught up in daily routines, requests, and urgencies. Unless you carve out a space for your goals or other activities you mean to do but never seem to have time for, they can easily get pushed aside. Building a bridge between your daily actions and those larger intentions occurs during regular and consistent planning.

In addition to the look ahead, **this Pillar includes a look back so you can analyze how you did, compared to your plan.** Many overlook this important step, yet it's critical to see and understand where you're prone to getting derailed and which activities take more or less time than you anticipate. A plan provides you with one place to reference for direction, resulting in improved self-management throughout the day. As you build an effective planning practice, it brings to light which systems and tools are most helpful and prompts a regular look at your goals so that you set them in motion. Even the Pillar of Arrangement is impacted when you schedule time for regular upkeep and maintenance of your workspaces, records, and information. If you recognize many of these as components of the other 5 Pillars, you are spot on! **The Planning Pillar has the greatest ability to impact and strengthen ALL the other Pillars.** What better reason do you need to start your work here?

The Benefits Of A Strong Planning Pillar

Focus often lands first on things we seek to improve or fix, ignoring those things that work well. It's true that the aim of this book is to provide insight and ways to address each Pillar when it's not as effective as it could be. Yet I also urge you to acknowledge where your strengths lie. Skills that come more easily or are frequently used tend to get discounted yet should be considered assets. What comes naturally to you may be something with which others struggle.

I've witnessed a shift in people's confidence when they realize the area or Pillar they're focused on improving represents only a portion of their overall capabilities regarding productivity. Better yet, people's strengths can translate into tools that help sharpen skills in other areas. When strength exists in the Planning Pillar, you are in a prime place to implement real change to improve your time management and productivity! With its ability to impact the other Pillars, it is powerful! Below are some examples.

You Know This Pillar Is Strong If...

You are ready to ACT.

Those who are strong in this area often begin the week with an anticipated pattern to their days and clearly understand their priorities and tasks. They are ready to launch as the week begins. A consistent routine of thorough planning results in a strategy for action. The decisions on what to do and how to get it accomplished happen when you are in a strategic mindset vs. a reactive one. Those who exhibit strength here do not need to allot their "prime time" each day to evaluate all there is to do and make decisions. Rather, you are ready to **work the plan** and simply need to look at where you left off and make course corrections to the plan as needed.

You can be Proactive vs. Reactive.

By its very nature, thinking ahead while you plan expands your line of sight from what is right in front of you into the future. The only way to become less reactive is to make this shift! Planning encompasses a view not only of the day ahead but of the weeks coming up. With that knowledge in mind, making quality choices about what the coming week can hold is possible. Those who consistently invest time to make purposeful decisions during planning are regularly looking down the road. They can see what's coming and decide what deserves their time and focus.

You make headway on your goals.

For some, goals are a driving force, keeping motivation high. For others, it takes more intentional work to carve out time to make progress on them. Regardless of where you fall, if you are strong in this Pillar, you can capitalize on planning as the time to regularly connect with your goals and take the next steps. Maintaining only those goals that remain important to you and keeping them front-of-mind is key to putting them in motion.

You give activities a home.

Strong planners consider all there is to get done and match it with the most effective rhythm for their days. You can carve out and assign the optimal time for tasks and projects as well as hold space for the unexpected. You're less likely to get derailed as new requests come your way. Unless there's a need for immediacy, it can be noted in your plan so that you remember to address it during the appropriate time.

You know what you DON'T have to do.

There is a bonus (or what I consider a by-product) when you assign a "home" in your day or week for activities. You've established when that work is going to happen—and when it's not. Many clients have shared with me their relief when they realize they don't have to do it NOW simply because it comes to mind. The self-discipline in this Pillar results in being able to let go of the feeling that "I have to do this now, so I don't forget."

How Does *Your* Planning Pillar Hold Up?

The term in engineering that addresses a structure's ability to support the load it was designed to hold is called "structural integrity." When cracks appear in a wall or pillar, the clues point to weakened stability or reliability. For the 6 Pillars, there are similar signs or indicators that there is more to investigate.

In my work, I've had many people share the personal impact resulting from their productivity struggles. They know how they **feel** and what they are **experiencing,** yet they may not know what to do to improve their situation. When I hear statements or emotions, such as the ones below, I see indicators that there is more to explore within the Pillar of Planning. Do you experience any of the following?

- Little or no planning occurs—you "hit the ground running" every day.
- There are goals or areas of work that are not given the time or attention they need.
- You rely on prompts, reminders, or approaching deadlines as your call to action.
- You do things NOW so that they won't be forgotten.

Days can get out of hand very quickly when you address items as they come up vs. having a predetermined set of priorities or intended tasks. Your habits may steer you to look through emails, have discussions with family or colleagues, opt to handle preferred tasks vs. important ones, or look up "just one more thing" online before getting started with the day. That churning of activity might be the default when there is no defined structure for your day, or you begin without a clear direction in mind.

Insufficient time for activities or little attention given to important focus areas that rarely get attention can signal two things: (1) There is a lack of structure that includes those activities and/or (2) Planning hasn't occurred to break down the next steps and get those scheduled. It's frustrating to feel that important goals or projects are regularly put on the back burner in order to address interruptions, other activities, or urgencies. Guilt also comes into play when the intent truly exists, but it's unclear HOW to give those things equal weight so they earn your time and attention amid all that can crop up during your week.

When no plan exists, there is often a heavy reliance on external prompts to get things done. We all want to feel that we won't forget important tasks or deadlines. So, our inclination can be to simply get it out of our heads and capture it in a way that will remind us to get it done. Lacking a designated time for activities, some will schedule a pop-up reminder or jot it on a post-it note. The alert then shows the deadline approaching, often when it is right around the corner, or perhaps that post-it note gets buried for days. And that's a problem when your reminder shows up at a time that isn't convenient to give your attention to the task. When you wait until the deadline is looming, it may mean working in crisis mode. Even if you ignore other work or obligations to focus solely on the urgency at hand, there may be inadequate time to do your best or most complete work.

The symptom of regularly doing tasks NOW so they won't be forgotten exists in two Pillars. Within the Planning Pillar, it can be a flag that the planning process is missing, meaning there is no time at which regular decision-making happens regarding *when* to get things done. If you don't have a way to make sure you can plan it for later, you better take care of it while it's top-of-mind, perpetuating the work style of "swatting flies"—when you deal with whatever flies before you. When planning becomes a regular activity, it simplifies what to do with those things that come up throughout the week—you either schedule it for an appropriate time during the week ahead, OR you capture the item and revisit it when you plan next. You'll also see this item as a symptom for the Resources Pillar as it can signal that there is no mechanism in place to store these items as they come up, so you remember and plan for them later. When you have a regular process to schedule your to-dos as well as a place or system to hold all those tasks, you can usually eliminate this symptom.

STRENGTHENING THE PLANNING PILLAR
TIPS & TECHNIQUES

Now, let's begin the work of strengthening and reinforcing the Planning Pillar. This section provides steps to take and a variety of options to choose from. Each step helps you progress through the work of improving your skills and honing techniques. I offer up alternative ways to approach the work of each step, but it is not necessary to try every single option provided. Consider this a menu from which you will pull out those approaches that feel most helpful to you. Some may be brand-new ideas for you; others may have been things you've done in the past. You may try some verbatim, or they may spark ideas for adapting it to fit your needs even better. The goal is to develop strength here, regardless of which methods and tactics you use.

Whether you need to start work on the Planning Pillar from the very beginning or wish to simply tweak or fine-tune your current planning process, this section is where "the rubber hits the road." Improvement begins now. Getting a clear picture of all the components that regularly need space in your week is the starting point. Step One helps you design a week with purpose. If you already have a regular pattern established for your days and weeks, you can still participate in this exercise to see if it sparks any new ideas, or you can skip ahead to "Step Two: Building a Planning Routine."

STEP 1
CREATE A SCHEDULE MODEL

A Schedule Model is simply a visual tool that reflects how you can strategically place all the various activities you need and want to build into your schedule. It has been eye-opening for clients as they work through the process to make all the components fit. Once complete, it can be used as a reference tool—a model—when planning. Even for individuals with a schedule that varies greatly from day to day or week to week, it can still be a beneficial exercise—just be sure to key in on the tips below about how to apply it with adaptations each week when planning. Below are steps and considerations as you create a Schedule Model that works for you.

Identify your key areas of responsibility.

There's an old saying—"the squeaky wheel gets the grease"—that often proves true when it comes to how and where we spend our time. Our attention is easily drawn to urgencies, requests, and deadlines. At the end of the day, you may realize that some important areas didn't get any of your attention since they weren't the "squeaky wheels." For this reason, we will begin this exercise by identifying the key parts of your life. To ensure that your Schedule Model includes the most valuable components, you must be able to capture and reflect on a complete list. If those are not clearly defined for you, or you wish to explore this more fully, the following questions may assist you in compiling an inventory.

What are your primary roles? These may be your job title or other roles, whether personal or professional. Some consume much of our time, while others require less time but are incredibly important. Are there any roles you wish to add now or in the future? Examples of roles that I've seen clients define include a family member (parent/spouse/child), supervisor, business owner, volunteer, caretaker, hobbyist, etc. You've likely identified many, so work to roll these up into a primary list. Another way to look at it would be to think about a pie chart. What are the main segments that fit together to make the whole? Does it reflect an accurate representation of your life as you wish it to be? Do any roles currently receive less time and attention than you'd like? Are any missing altogether?

What are the tasks and activities that fall under each role? Set a timer for three minutes and create an exhaustive list of the activities that support your primary roles. How do you currently fit them into your schedule?

What activities deserve regular, recurring time in your schedule? Within your key roles are the activities and categories of work that support those areas of responsibility. For example, a role such as "business owner" covers many areas. Perhaps much time is spent on managing staff and handling client work, but marketing gets less focus than it requires.

Are there any themes? Activities may have similarities by nature of the type of work at hand (returning emails/calls, updating client/patient records, household maintenance, social media, and marketing posts, etc.) OR they may be grouped by category (marketing, operations, client services, leadership/management, etc.) These themes can prove helpful when you schedule that work.

Are there activities that don't get the attention they should? Consider those things that don't tend to make it onto your calendar or plan yet take time in your day. Email often comes up here with my clients as it can consume their time but is often not reflected on their calendars or considered when planning tasks for the day. Deep Focus activities, covered earlier, also fall victim to this. Those activities aren't as tangible and may have no definitive finish line, such as strategic thinking, leadership development, continuing education, planning/preparation, etc., so they may continually be placed on the back burner.

What items tend to get overlooked altogether? Think about things that frequently get pushed off or ignored altogether. Are they truly less important? Or do you need to consider them when deciding how to allocate your time?

Consider your GOALS. One of the first steps to move goals from being dreams to reality is to get strategic. Target space and reserve room for the work to happen. We will walk through exercises in the coming chapters to help you think about and clarify the goals you want to achieve. Once you identify them, allotting time in your schedule gives them a "home" where they can receive your attention and work.

You may feel overwhelmed at this point as you've created many roles to act on, tasks that need to get done, and goals to bring to fruition. Not to fear! Set these lists aside for the moment while we consider the next step in building your schedule model.

Develop a "Time Strategy."

Before you begin to fill your calendar with activities, this is the time for you to think tactically about *how* you work best. Our schedules can quickly fill up, with little thought given to where those activities rightfully belong. How can you maximize your focus and energy on the work that needs it most? Can you make a plan for where and when to schedule meetings or projects so that they don't eat into prime time for other work? While we can't always control how things get scheduled or where activities land, we CAN influence it by creating a strategy for our time. As you start to picture your ideal week, consider the following:

When do you concentrate best? Some people are morning people, others are night owls, and some kick it into gear in the afternoons. Regardless of your preference, do you utilize your most mindful time for those activities that require a high level of focus or creativity? **This time is the prime real estate** in your day. How can you hold this space so you use it wisely and it doesn't fall prey to minutiae and activities that could be done elsewhere in your schedule?

When is your energy lowest? Everyone has a time of day when they feel more sluggish or lack focus. That doesn't mean it needs to be wasted. You can still be productive when you plan that time to do tasks that have a higher level of interaction or engagement. Deep Focus work can be a challenge during low-energy times in your day, but more dynamic tasks fit the bill. Activities where you move physically and/or interact with others fit well here, such as organizing, data entry, errands, and returning emails/calls. Meetings where you are a participant (vs. a passive listener) can also be considered active. Can you place these at times in your schedule when you tend to have less energy so that they generate a pick-me-up and leave your best focus time for other things?

Where can you establish more influence over your time? As I do with my clients, I challenge you to look at your schedule with a critical eye. Almost everyone has items on their calendar that are non-negotiable, yet I'll bet some fall within your area of influence and ability to offer different options. Don't overlook your ability to offer up alternative times for things or shift a schedule just because it's become routine. Part of this exercise is to broaden your options. Are there things handled in person that could be done virtually or via email more easily? Could you establish blocks of time that are held for targeted work (think Deep Focus, projects, communication, etc.) and will not be offered up for appointments unless truly needed? Can you identify a portion of your schedule that is yours alone to schedule so that a colleague or even family member cannot book that time without your input? Weigh what you know about your own work style and preferences against what your Schedule Model is already reflecting. Where you see a disconnect, ask what IS possible to improve it. Establish a model for how you offer up your time to others and where you need to hold it open for your own priorities.

How do you prefer to have your schedule spaced out? Beyond the tasks and meetings, consider the pace at which you work best. Do you prefer back-to-back meetings/appointments with larger blocks of unstructured time on other days? Or do you find it best to space meetings out so that you have a few scheduled commitments each day or room in between to regroup or capture notes? Can you arrange errands, client appointments, and meetings on certain days to maximize travel time and mileage? Do blocks of time between scheduled activities lend themselves well to a specific activity? This is a step where I encourage you to get creative. Think outside the box and come up with new ideas about "how" you can work; begin to build a plan aligned with the flow that feels right for you. Try out a few variations and note how that flow works for you. It helps you home in on a rhythm that feels most natural.

Start with a blank weekly calendar template.

We're now ready to get tactical and design your model! It's best to begin with a clean slate. To give you an idea of a layout to use, I've provided a simple template in the Appendix at the back of this book, but a blank weekly calendar or a simple sheet of paper can work as well. Make sure it encompasses the hours of your full day, from the time your day typically starts to where it ends.

For some of you, life and work may follow a rhythm different than a traditional Monday-Friday role. Examples are those whose days off are Monday and Tuesday so that their week "begins" on Wednesday morning, someone whose work rotation spans multiple weeks before beginning again, or an individual who has various bi-weekly meetings occurring at different times each week. If this sounds like you, your schedule model can begin on the day you feel best represents the start of your week. It may even consist of multiple weeks, so the varying flow of activity can be plotted out most accurately. Really, there is no one way it must appear—it only needs to represent a container of time that you feel is appropriate to you and your routines.

Plot out regularly recurring activities.

You'll begin by adding those things that already have a timeslot on your calendar. In a sense, a Schedule Model is a blueprint for your time, and recurring activities are like the "columns in the room" —those things you need to work around. These may be standing appointments but can also signify routines or activities that already have a regular space in your day, such as drop-off times for school-age children, office hours, commute times, times for medications, scheduled breaks, standing meetings, or other regularly performed tasks. I recommend adding non-work activities even if your main goal is to create a structure focused more on work. They should be reflected and fully considered when looking at how they impact your week. They require a portion of your physical and mental energy, as well as impact the availability you have for other activities. You may fill multiple roles, but you're still ONE person, and your capacity needs to be taken into consideration, as these roles and responsibilities all pull from within you.

Where are you spending your time now? Look beyond the scheduled meetings and what has been on your calendar. Think about what activities consume your time and where they happen. Are there areas where you spend an inordinate amount of time on something that should not be such a prime activity? Where are there inefficiencies?

What do you NEVER seem to have time for? What are your often-overlooked or frequently "back-burnered" activities? Weed through these to discern which truly are valuable and which may be ideas or projects that no longer draw you or have lessened in importance over time. Which items deserve time but may rarely get it?

How much structure vs. flexibility is needed? Consider what the outcome of your Schedule Model would look like so that it is most realistic and helpful to YOU. Does a model that is dense with activity or one with room to maneuver and react feel more useful and practical? What level of responsiveness is in your role? In other words, what is the degree to which you are called to respond and address unscheduled things that come into your day? To best illustrate different levels of responsiveness, see the following examples of two extremes:

Low Responsiveness

Barry is an executive coach who works from his home-based office. He has regularly scheduled coaching appointments via phone each day. He is a solopreneur, so he handles all marketing, networking, and operations and addresses emails and calls from prospective clients throughout the day. There are a lot of things he handles, and he is busy every day, all day. However, he can return calls and emails when he is able and works to schedule the other activities throughout the week. There is the occasional urgency when he needs to address a client issue or pull together a speaking proposal that was requested on short notice. Overall, **the level of responsiveness required in Barry's role is low** since he rarely has items come up unexpectedly that can take over his day.

High Responsiveness

Charles is a Junior Planner at a financial advisory firm. He is working alongside a Senior Planner at the firm on two client projects involving client outreach and processing applications and paperwork. Part of the Junior Planner's role is to help with phone coverage by answering the main phone line, directing calls, and addressing general questions. Charles ends up fielding an average of four to five calls each hour. Some are simple and take only minutes. Others mean checking to see if documentation has been received or clarifying information needed, which can take much more time. **The level of responsiveness needed in Charles' role is high.** When building his plan for the day, he should always consider that each hour will likely be impacted by the need to be responsive to the calls he receives. It isn't that these calls conflict with his role—they are part of his role.

Ultimately, the level of detail in your Schedule Model should be based on both the responsiveness of your role(s) as well as how full or open you prefer it to be. Aim for a balance between enough detail to

> be comprehensive yet flexible enough to acknowledge the fluidity of your days. So, for those with a low need for responsiveness in their role and who prefer having their day clearly defined, a detailed, comprehensive Structure Model may be for you. For those who may not enjoy the idea of structure but recognize its value in aiding us to accomplish what needs to get done, you can create a Structure Model that is much more open and flexible. In the case of Charles above, he has a high level of responsiveness in that he can be required to switch focus and respond to an issue as part of his role. How he structures and defines his time needs to allow more fluidity than in the example of Barry, who has more control over how things impact his daily plan and routine. Examples of several client Schedule Models are also included in the Appendix at the back of the book to provide a look at the different formats these can take based on different roles and work styles.

Block portions of your day for tasks or categories of work/focus.

As a building's blueprint defines specific areas for different purposes, our days can be designed in a similar fashion. Your Schedule Model should currently hold only those scheduled activities you added earlier. Now it's time to flesh out what your Schedule Model can look like by filling in the gaps in your scheduled activities. Using your list of roles, responsibilities, and activities, begin to space out actions so that they have a home in your schedule. Some thoughts as you begin to sketch out the possibilities:

- Some entries may be specific—i.e., designating certain times to check and respond to emails. Others may be broad—i.e., working on marketing activities each Wednesday afternoon or education/industry reading each morning before email.

Pillar 1: Planning

- Only make it as detailed as you feel is needed to capture the main areas.

- Don't fill it entirely unless your level of responsiveness in your role is low and you enjoy structure.

- Leave enough room to be flexible when needed yet specific enough to provide a home for important activities. New tasks will come in, and some things will take longer to complete than you anticipated. It's a good idea to have room to absorb them into your week.

- You'll likely need to fine-tune your Schedule Model over time, so don't try to make it perfect. In the first weeks, ask, "what am I missing?" Are there regular tasks and activities that you didn't factor in? Do some areas need more time than you thought they'd require? What needs to shift or change once you see the schedule model in action?

- If you find visual cues helpful, you may opt to use color or other ways to designate between various activities: some examples are personal items in blue, meetings/appointments in red, admin work vs. projects/tasks in green, etc. The goal is to make it easy to review quickly and get a sense of the types of activities on the schedule and where they fall.

The final product is a RESOURCE. It does not mean that the weeks won't vary from this structure; it simply provides a road map for where and how regular activities can fit in. It will also help you know what needs to be moved and planned elsewhere when changes to your schedule come up. In the next section on Planning, you'll learn ways to reference your Schedule Model during the planning process.

STEP 2
DEVELOP A PLANNING ROUTINE

Planning is the backbone of productivity, and while it is simple in theory, it shouldn't be mistaken for "simplistic." This activity does the most to reach out and support all the other Pillars and make a positive impact when done thoroughly. If you view planning only as a time to prioritize a list of tasks that are already top-of-mind, it limits the scope and insight it can provide. At a high level, planning is all about making strategic DECISIONS.

Designate Planning as a high-value activity.

Looking at your schedule, tasks, goals, and other considerations are vital if you are to intentionally build a road map for the coming days. Too often, planning gets relegated to the first few minutes of the day when the pressures of commitments are already on top of us. That means we are easily swayed by distractions, urgencies, and even our mood or attitude. If you remove the planning process from a time of day when you are getting ready to hit the ground running, you can place it at a time when you can better strategize with logic vs. emotions. As you determine when to do a task, you will make better choices when you aren't filtering it through thoughts of whether you feel like doing it NOW. Below are steps to build an effective planning routine:

Establish a consistent time for planning each week.

Some like to launch their week by planning, while others I've known enjoy planning for the upcoming week as they wrap up the current week. There is no right or wrong way to do this—it simply needs to be consistent and feel like the most natural timing to you. Be sure that you assign planning to a time when you are in the right frame of mind for strategic thinking and won't be distracted. Select a part of the day when you have high energy and feel ready to connect with your goals/projects at hand. Once you are in the habit, planning can take as little as 15-20 minutes but will likely require more time as you begin. Schedule this block of time to plan on your calendar so that nothing lands in its space. You may feel tempted to sacrifice this time to pressing needs but make this time sacred. Few activities require so little investment of time for such a big payoff when done well.

Have the right tools & information on hand.

Nothing will throw a plan out the window faster than the realization after the fact that there were things you overlooked, therefore, failed to include. Look across your entire landscape of tasks, calendars, goals, deadlines, and roles to avoid that pitfall. When you plan, lift yourself above the day-to-day work and take a 360° scan of everything that impacts your time and attention. The need to access all that information may end up dictating where and when you do your planning each week. You can't plan at the kitchen table if most of your info is at the office or vice versa. Here are a few things to have available so you can plan thoroughly:

Your calendar AND other calendars that impact yours. Your team/department calendar, school calendar, a spouse's/family calendar, organizations in which you participate or volunteer, etc.

Tasks. You will want to have access to the main places you receive, capture, and track tasks and to-dos. Do you keep a master list of things you want to accomplish? Do you utilize a task management system or app for tracking items? All these places where we store tasks and activities are your capture tools. Also, consider the ways tasks enter your world from external sources—paper, email, task management software, notes from meetings, etc.

Goals. Planning is the time when you weave your personal goals into your day-to-day activity. (More will be covered in an upcoming section about identifying and documenting your goals.) The key to integrating them into your time is to get them out of your head, define the steps you'll take to accomplish them, and then give them visibility as you would your everyday tasks. Invite them to take up residence alongside your work and existing activities and routines.

Your planning system. Whether you use paper, electronic, or a blend of both, you'll want a system or tool to hold and track your plan. Don't rely solely on your memory. A planning system provides a visual reminder of your plan, giving you a dashboard from which to operate. It helps you monitor progress and adjust as plans change. You can also use it to capture new things that come up throughout the week. If you do not currently use any kind of planning system, I suggest you begin with paper as it is easiest to implement and adapt. A sample weekly planning sheet is available in the Appendix. We will cover more about planning systems in the section on Resources.

Look at the coming week—then extend your view at least two weeks further.

The only way to move from reactive to proactive is to extend your view beyond today or tomorrow, which means you must build a regular routine of looking ahead in time to see what is coming up in your schedule. The first thing this does is give you a sense of how the upcoming weeks will flow—which days are busier, where there is open space to work on tasks, and where the schedule varies from your normal routine. It also allows you to see what deliverables are on the horizon to determine what may need to happen in the current week to make progress toward those deadlines.

Reference your Schedule Model.

If you built a Schedule Model (see "Step One" earlier in this section) to identify how to best structure your time, compare it to your calendar for the coming days. Does the coming week lend itself to assigning activities as you determined optimal in your model? If things conflict, what needs to move, and where can it now occur? Will anything need to be put on hold for a later week? It could be that some items will not earn a place in the coming week, yet it's still important to reference the Schedule Model as it is the framework you built that made sure to include all the most vital activities you intend to invest time in. Adjust your Schedule Model as you learn more about your work style and needs.

Note meetings and deadlines in your planning system.

If using an electronic calendar, your schedule may already be in place, but if you are using a paper planning system, transfer these details to your planning page. It can feel like duplicate work, but I hear time and again how valuable it is to see and be reminded of your schedule throughout the day. Have these scheduled events in place first so you can identify the fixtures in that week around which everything else must fit. Once those are in place, you can choose which non-time-specific actions and tasks you plan to accomplish and where they will fit.

Notice the flow of the week ahead.

Which days/times are filled with appointments or meetings? Where do you have chunks of time open to work on projects or tasks? After assessing their schedule, I ask clients to tell me about their "container of time" for the coming week. We quantify how much time exists for which they will be able to plan activities. We look at where there are busy vs. open times in the week and determine how much time remains available. When you back out scheduled appointments, travel time, breaks, etc., how much time is left? Are there days with a very limited container of time? Which days are wide open or have "chunks" of time available for use? That awareness is needed as you begin making choices and focusing on your activities.

Look at the previous week to see what wasn't completed.

One of the most frequently overlooked aspects of planning—and something that I find critical to growth and improvement, is to reflect on progress from the week behind you. There is a wealth of knowledge in looking back at what got accomplished, what didn't (and why), and what trends emerged. What can be learned from examining how you navigated the week? Many task apps simply "bulldoze" items forward when they are not completed on the designated day. Sometimes that may be appropriate—you didn't complete it yesterday, and now, it *must* get done today. However, don't assume that's the case. You may have other things that take priority in the days ahead, or your schedule may already be full. Make choices on anything you feel should be set aside until you plan for an upcoming week. Just be sure to capture them in a place where you will be sure to revisit them later. Planning is a time for you to reset: to close out the prior week, move forward any tasks that remains outstanding, and make your choices for the coming week. You don't want to derail your current plan by later realizing you ALSO have incomplete items from last week that you forgot to consider.

Select the tasks you intend to address in the coming week.

Task selection usually comprises much of the time spent when people plan. After the full reflection above, it's time for the purposeful work of selecting the most relevant and highest priority activities you'll work on and determining where that work will happen. Consider the following:

Look at deadlines. The obvious tasks will be those tied to an upcoming deliverable or due date. Look at those due for the coming week, but also in the next two weeks. Are there steps you can take on those now?

Get specific. Use your Schedule Model. Look at chunks of time you've designated for a specific type of work. Do you have sections of your week/day set aside for staff development, admin work, marketing, or even family events? Select the specific activities you'll be working on when you reach those scheduled times. Predetermining tasks helps reduce the chance of procrastination or feeling overwhelmed when you get there so that you don't have to rely on making choices at a time when you are ready to act. Even if you need to adjust your week and move your focus time to another day, you can do that and select tasks during planning.

Act on your goals. This is how you make those dreams and goals a reality. What activity, task, or thinking can you do in the coming days to move those forward? Not every week may have time for goal work, but it's still important to put them front-of-mind during planning so that you are sure to stay connected with them. You may even opt to reserve a block in your Schedule Model to have time for those goals regularly.

Be realistic about how much you can do in one day. It may take time to develop this skill. Remember the level of "responsiveness" in your role as well as the container of time available, as discussed earlier. Realize also that people tend to underestimate how much time it will take to work on tasks. There is always transition time between activities, interruptions, and additional requests coming your way, as well as a flow of communication and emails that you need to balance with those things you had already scheduled. A good starting place can be one of the following:

- Cap the number of tasks you assign yourself (i.e., no more than five a day).
- List those things you hope to get done. Then cut that list by 30%.
- Flag one or two top priorities, highlighting their value and making it harder to bypass them for other lower-priority tasks.

Daily, review the plan and "course correct" as needed.

Since we've positioned detailed planning as an activity that happens weekly instead of daily, you shouldn't have to go back to the drawing board each day to make decisions about what today will hold. The choices have already been made. **Your focus as the day starts is to first reference the plan; second, work the plan; and third, adjust when necessary.** Things will come up throughout the week where you need to make judgment calls. Do you move something you had planned to do today to take on a new activity that came up yesterday? Have priorities changed so that tasks need to be moved? Has there been a delay or problem which held up something you'd intended to work on? Unless changes mean that your entire plan needs to be overhauled, daily planning may only require a quick perusal before moving ahead. More will be covered on this later in "Pillar 4—Leveraging your Habits & Self-Management."

Implement a planning tool for tracking both time and tasks.

While much more will be covered on this topic in "Pillar 6—Resources," I have included in the Appendix a blank planning page you can begin using if you do not currently have a system that works for you. For now, I offer some thoughts to consider as you decide how to best capture and monitor your plan:

Consider your abilities and preferences (technology vs. paper planners, apps, etc.) If unsure, think about how you typically capture things you need to remember or do. Do you default to writing it down, or would you grab your phone/computer to capture it online? If you don't have a consistent tool yet, I recommend starting with a simple paper system rather than waiting to decide on the perfect one. I tell my clients, let's work on the process first. Finding the right tool comes second.

Tailor it to your needs. Some people need a lot of room to schedule meetings, appointments, etc. Others need more space to take notes or create lists. Start considering what you need to have at your fingertips as it relates to maintaining and effectively working your plan.

Capture BOTH your schedule AND to-dos effectively. A planning system may be a combo of technology and paper, OR both may be housed in the same tool, such as Outlook or Asana. It's incredibly useful to have the ability to reference your calendar alongside your planned activities. Working solely from a calendar is only successful when every activity is scheduled for a specific time. Most of us need multiple ways to track and monitor all that goes into our time.

STEP 3
ADAPTING WHEN THE PLAN CHANGES

It's inevitable. Plans change despite our best intentions. In fact, it's a rare thing for a week to play out 100% as you anticipate. We underestimate how long things take, illnesses knock people out of commission, flights get canceled, commitments by others aren't met, or a fantastic opportunity that is worth shifting gears to accommodate can come up. Regardless, you can be highly productive even when the week plays out differently than you intended. Working through these changes and opportunities is the management portion of Time Management. You should consider your productivity skills to be active. It's how you navigate, adjust, and accommodate change. In nature, a rigid tree might snap during heavy winds, but a thin sapling can weather the storm more easily because it's able to bend and snap back. Let's consider ways you can react to those changes and remain pliable to the winds that come your way.

Daily planning is one activity that helps gauge progress and identify where we need to adapt. While weekly planning is where strategy and decisions occur, **daily planning is where we make modifications and adjustments so that our plan stays relevant, practical, and productive.** As you begin your day, start with a look at the weekly plan. What needs to be added? What needs to move to accommodate change? What may need to be rescheduled? Where might you need to expedite a task?

Prepare yourself to accommodate plan changes by considering the following:

- **Does it warrant adding to your plan this week?** Rather than tossing the plan altogether, evaluate the current plan to determine if it gets added or if you can address it later. Just because you get a request today, it may not mean you have to respond immediately to someone else's urgency. Clarify deadlines and confirm turnarounds to ensure you don't assume a quick turnaround is required. Propose a completion date that works with your plan, if possible. The first question when a change comes up is, "Does it belong in this week?" Then, work to accommodate as needed.

- **Where can you capture info, tasks, or requests that come up?** The influx of things to do doesn't stop once we plan. Having a reliable place to capture new, incoming requests and deliverables helps you safely hold those activities until an appropriate time to do them. Otherwise, you may find yourself regularly interrupting work to handle things *NOW*, so you won't forget to do it *LATER*.

- **How will you accommodate and leave room for changes**? Have you built enough room in your schedule to allow space for additional tasks that come your way? Discipline yourself to avoid planning a heavily packed schedule.

- **What is worthy of changing your plan?** Do requests from a boss or client always need to go to the top of the list? Can you say "no" more often to tasks that fall outside your area of responsibility? Where can you set a guideline for what you will allow to alter your plan vs. those you'll schedule at a later, more opportune time?

You may be great at crafting a weekly plan, but without the skills to adapt when changes occur, you're susceptible to changes hijacking your week. Think ahead about how to become nimbler about modifying your plan when needed. More will be covered on this in later chapters.

PLANNING
KEY TAKEAWAYS

This Pillar is about being purposeful with when, where, and how you choose to direct your focus and energy. It looks at the architecture of your time and how to be most efficient.

Schedule Model

- Developing a schedule model is both an exercise AND a resource.
- Drafting your model week helps you think through how you can best make all the categories fit. It assigns homes to activities and serves as a reminder to build in time for those often overlooked, but important actions.
- Consider the best placement of activities so that you can capitalize on your best focus time for work that requires concentration and creativity.
- Even if your weeks vary in how they play out, a Schedule Model can be a resource and reference to use so that you regularly include those roles and activities that are most valuable.

Planning

- This activity has the most impact of any other activity and can help support ALL the other Pillars.
- Make this a regular, weekly routine. This investment of time is vital! Have access to the information that will help you plan most appropriately (calendars, tasks, projects, etc.)
- Make decisions on the intended work for the coming week. Operate from a higher level of oversight so you can focus more strategically on what you should set out to do. Create a plan you can use as you move through your week. Reference it regularly as you would a blueprint when building.

- Planning should incorporate a look across all categories of your life. Pull forward any tasks you didn't accomplish last week so that you don't need to look "back in time" for direction.
- Extend your view beyond today and tomorrow. Plan for this week, but look ahead at the next two to see what is coming and if work is needed now for any deliverables coming up.

Develop techniques to change the Plan

- Daily planning is time to reflect on the plan you made at the start of the week. It is a chance to reset and refresh it to incorporate changes that happened the day prior.
- Where will you capture things to do that come up? If they can't be handled this week, note them so you can revisit them during next week's planning.
- When something happens to upset the plan, look first to the plan itself to see what needs to be adjusted.
- Based on how responsive your role, you may need to build in more open space and flexibility so that your plan allows room for those last-minute changes. The higher your responsiveness, the more flexible your schedule needs to be.

PILLAR 2
INTERNAL TIME CLOCK

How often do you lose track of time? Does it happen only occasionally, or is it a regular occurrence? What happens when you're working "in the zone" on a project? Can you sense when it's time to move on to something else? Or do you get so hyper-focused that everything else fades into the background? Focused concentration is great unless you wind up dedicating far too much time to a task or it causes you to miss appointments, deadlines, or even meals.

Do you find yourself busy all day, every day, but can't really say what you spent your time doing? Maybe you're a habitual multi-tasker, or new responsibilities have been added to your world. Planning is hard without fully recognizing how much time your activities and routines truly take to complete!

How about sensing where you are timewise in your day? Some people can instinctively feel what time it is without even looking at the clock. Others find themselves surprised that it's 3:00 p.m. when they thought it was closer to midday. Which one are you?

The skills within this Pillar have to do with how you recognize, quantify, and allot time. Are you conscious of the passage of time in relation to your activities? **This Pillar is about time awareness.** Several factors may impact that awareness. When these are weak or lacking, the result reduces our ability to be productive.

Knowing how much time your tasks require

How realistic are you at estimating the amount of time it takes to DO a task? It sounds straightforward, but components can be overlooked. In addition to our common tendency to *over*estimate the time we think is needed for those dreaded tasks, we often *under*estimate the time more straightforward activities require. A single to-do on your list may, in fact, take multiple steps to complete. Some tasks require preparation, training, or even research before the actual work begins. Are you factoring that in? For some activities, you may struggle to know the time requirement because it's a new task, you do it infrequently, or past multi-tasking hasn't allowed a clear opportunity to learn just how long it takes to complete on its own.

Feeling the passage of time

The second factor at play is an internal and instinctive one. It is what helps you stay in tune with where you are, timewise, in your day. Some refer to this as your **"internal clock."** When your internalized sense of time is weak, it could be due to lack of use. If there hasn't been a need or priority to stay tuned in to time, your abilities may not be sharp. As with any other skill, people are differently abled. What comes naturally for some, others find less intuitive. Additionally, ADHD or other brain-based conditions can hinder one's sense of time and its passage. This section provides techniques to address both elements so this Pillar—your Internal Time Clock—can strongly support your productivity.

Valuing time

One additional aspect is worth mentioning. How is time *valued* by you and those around you? Different cultures, regions, and even organizations have their own approach to and attitude toward time. You've likely experienced places where life feels like time moves at a different pace than your norm, whether faster or slower. Work and play are intertwined for some. Others have clearly defined boundaries between the two. Even the concept of being "on time" means something quite different to different people. Understanding where values about time are at play will help you identify what is appropriate for you, your environment, and those with whom you interact.

For some of you, a great focus on time awareness and your Internal Time Clock may not be vital, and that's OK. Some people live more insular lives and don't need to intertwine their work and rhythms with others. Others may thrive in that creative zone—or "flow"—and have the capacity to stay there as long as possible. The question is how much weight this Pillar needs to support you in your world. It is worth analyzing it to see if it is impacting your ability to:

- achieve what you set out to accomplish
- meet commitments and deadlines, and
- plan your use of time appropriately

THE BENEFITS OF A STRONG INTERNAL TIME CLOCK PILLAR

If you are someone who finds the skills in this Pillar come naturally, it might be a surprise to learn that many people do struggle with their Internal Time Clock. In fact, results from my 6 Pillars assessment flag this Pillar most frequently as one needing to be addressed. So, for those of you blessed with an intuitive sense of time awareness, these are ways you can capitalize on that strength.

YOU KNOW THIS PILLAR IS STRONG IF......

Your planning is realistic.

Your ability to approximate and budget time works in your favor as you plan how much you aim to get done in your days or weeks. Since a wildly unrealistic task list is one of the easiest ways to derail your day, having the skills to make your plan more attainable means you are starting from a more manageable place. You understand the need to prioritize. Low time awareness can lead to putting *everything* on your to-do list because "it all needs to get done" rather than facing the reality that the amount of time you have in a day is limited, and you'll need to make choices to only plan for those things that are attainable.

You are dependable with deadlines and timeliness.

This area of strength is an asset as you make commitments. You have the knowledge to understand when deliverables are attainable and when they aren't. Setting appropriate expectations and communicating them well translates to others considering you reliable.

You stay on target.

Time awareness will monitor where you are in your day and how much time you have spent (and may still need to spend) on tasks, which means you can use this strength in your favor to catch yourself if you start to get derailed or find your plan needs to be adjusted when things take more or less time than expected.

You can pace your work more naturally.

Since your natural sense of time and time requirements are at play when you queue up work to do, you may find yourself better able to pace your work which means that you have the skills to enjoy a less harried pace.

You are less likely to get over-committed.

Having a strong sense of a task's time requirement means you can plan more appropriately and sense when the volume is exceeding your limits. Skills in this area help you recognize the red flags of a daily or weekly plan that is no longer realistic; team that with good self-management skills to take appropriate action, communicate your limits, and amend your plan when needed—a valuable gift to possess!

HOW WELL DOES *YOUR* INTERNAL TIME CLOCK HOLD UP?

As you've read the scenarios throughout this section, did any of them sound familiar to you? Do you have a sense of whether this is a Pillar of strength or if you need reinforcement here? Another way to gauge your needs is to consider some of the situations below to see if you are experiencing them in your own world.

- Hyper-focusing
- Perpetually running late
- Consistently trying to fit too many tasks or activities into a specified time
- Unrealistic task lists
- Feelings of low self-esteem

A frequent challenge I hear voiced by clients is losing track of time when working on something. It's no rare thing to get absorbed in a task or project and spend more time on it than you anticipated. It happens to everyone from time to time. What IS problematic is when it becomes so frequent that the amount of time being spent means regularly sacrificing part of your day that you had allotted elsewhere; when saying yes to one activity results in saying no to other activities which may be just as important—perhaps more so. That extra time spent may also be disproportional to the value of that task. Hyper-focusing can result in large amounts of time spent over-analyzing or researching, missing commitments, losing sleep, missing meals, and can even impact relationships.

Do you know anyone who is always running late? For some, the idea of being on time is only a mere suggestion. It harkens back to the way we each value the need to be on time. For others, the goal of arriving "on time" is impacted by miscalculating how long it would take to get where you need to be. Additionally, an overall naivete around everything that needs to be done in preparation to depart, the urge to do "just one more thing" before leaving, or underestimating drive/transition time are common hurdles as well.

As mentioned earlier, this Pillar is impacted by both knowledge of the time required for activities AND our internal sense of time. Lacking a strong combination of both makes it hard to be on target with how much you can aim to get done within the confines of any one day or week. Many err on the side of planning far too many things for the allotted time, otherwise known as the "planning fallacy" (the 1970s term coined by psychologists Kahneman and Tversky). Even those typically strong in time awareness can fall prey to the common truth that activities we dread will "feel" larger, and we assume they will take larger amounts of time than often proves true. On the other hand, we tend to underestimate things we approach with anything from neutral emotions to excitement. To be consistently unrealistic leads to feelings of inadequacy and guilt—real frustration results when, despite planning, you're unable to stay on track or to get things done. The emotional toll is high when this Pillar is weak. The good news is there are steps you can take to brace and fortify this Pillar, and the payoff can be huge!

CALIBRATING YOUR INTERNAL TIME CLOCK
TIPS & TECHNIQUES

Unique to this Pillar is that it's less about *what* you are doing and more about *how* you are internalizing and tracking what you are doing. Difficulty with time awareness means your internal prompts may be unreliable in nudging you back on course. So, we'll begin with establishing some external prompts that pull your awareness back to the usage of time. **Just as you might look periodically at a compass if you were hiking without a clear trail, you can build habits to regularly check in with time, monitor progress, and determine if you are on track or need to adjust your trajectory.** As you build your skills of time awareness and strengthen your Internal Time Clock, they will aid your accuracy with both planning and staying on track.

STEP 1
SET MILE MARKERS

We begin by looking at how to build a pace or gait into your days. When there's a measured rhythm, it's easier to track where you are in the day and how much time has elapsed. You begin to draw a line between what a span of time "feels" like and how much you can accomplish within it. To illustrate this idea of "feeling" time, think about a common activity you engage in that usually falls within a predictable length of time. Examples might be a movie or series episode, songs on the radio, a favorite podcast, a sermon, or typical wait time at your favorite restaurant after ordering your meal. When those run longer than average, you may have had a slight realization that "Wow, this movie is long!" or "That was shorter than usual." You can use that same skill of awareness and develop it for use throughout your day. You'll begin to internalize what it feels like to focus for 45 minutes on a project or when you have reached your lunch break. A few ideas to put this into action are below. Select one or two that feel most natural to implement.

Establish routine times of day for specific actions.

Think of a few activities that happen daily. Whether it's a wake-up alarm, when you depart for work/school, check email, take a walk, or return phone calls—commit to a set time for that to occur. Once established, do them regularly, at that set time, for at least two weeks. Small adjustments might be needed in the first day or two to make things workable. You can space these out, implementing one routine in the morning, another mid-morning or midday, another in the afternoon, and perhaps one more in the evening. The process helps you set guideposts that you'll pass throughout your day, which can raise your time awareness.

At the end of the day or week, reflect on how these worked for you. What surprised you? Are there parts of the day that feel as if they pass more slowly or quickly than you realized? These routines may evolve into habits when done frequently enough to build neural pathways. When that happens, you don't need as many external prompts to serve as reminders. They also help you internalize time through their continuity.

Utilize chimes at intervals.

My memories take me back to my grandparents' house. They had a clock that chimed the hour as well as partial chimes at 15-minute intervals. That clock could be heard in many areas throughout the house, and I recall hearing it chime faintly in the distance. I'd mentally log the time, then get back to whatever I had been doing beforehand. It didn't serve to prompt me unless I had somewhere to be or something to do that was coming up. What it did was provide me reminders that gave me mental mile markers. You can use this same technique to build time awareness. Chimes or alerts ringing every 15 minutes likely won't help, but perhaps fewer notices could serve the purpose. Perhaps hourly or at times such as mid-morning, lunchtime, mid-afternoon, and end-of-day would be helpful. My fitness watch notifies me at 10 till the hour if I haven't gotten up and walked, so it serves as a prompt for my time in addition to the healthy habit of moving frequently. Where could you set up a few reminders to mentally note the time and begin to internalize it?

Look to the sky.

If you work or spend a lot of time in windowless rooms or offices, periodically moving somewhere with access to a window or the outdoors can be helpful. Daylight looks different throughout the day and can help pace where you are in the day timewise.

Use apps and notifiers to alert you of the time or provide task reminders.

Where can you enlist some tools and applications to begin building regularity in your routine? Whether using the ideas listed above or other methods you find helpful, setting up prompts and reminders can be beneficial. When time awareness is an issue, you often cannot rely on your mindfulness to remember to do activities at specific times. Use external tools to give you that support.

STEP 2

MAKE THE PASSAGE OF TIME "RELATABLE"

The term "time blindness" is a good descriptor of what some people experience when it's hard to decipher not only the approximate time of day but also the relative speed at which they are moving through it. Techniques to make time relatable help create a better sense of the passage of time.

Analog clocks

One of the first tips I recommend is switching over to analog clocks from digital. Digital is a quick snapshot of time—where you are now. Analog clocks, with hour and minute hands, allow a visual representation of time's passage. Go back to using a good old-fashioned dial-face wristwatch or set up your smartwatch or Fitbit to display the time with an analog display. Update or change out as many clocks around you as you can, which is also a good tool for children as they begin to learn and "feel" time. Unfortunately, some phones may no longer have the capability to view an analog display, so it's even more important to find other tools to rely on to tell time.

Timers

Timers are great for breaking down work into smaller chunks of time. When you focus specifically on building time awareness, I recommend you select a time increment that you'll keep consistent (i.e., 20, 30, 45, or 60 minutes). The longer you work in those consistent segments of time, the more tuned in you will become to what that quantity of time feels like and how much you can accomplish within it. You may realize that time moves much more quickly than you originally thought, or you may find that you are able to get more done than you anticipated. This simple strategy does a lot to strengthen your internal clock as well as become more realistic about task length. A common application of this technique is Francesco Cirillo's "Pomodoro Technique." He recommends you segment work into intervals of 25 minutes followed by a five-minute break. Those intervals are called Pomodoros (Italian for tomato), named after the tomato-shaped timer he used when he developed the technique.

Another timer option is TimeTimer®. A great visual tool, TimeTimer® is laid out like a typical timer but displays in red the amount of time remaining to count down. As time counts down, the red color diminishes. So, a full hour is completely red, but by the time only 15 minutes remain, only a quarter of the timer's face is red. A simple glance can show you how much time is remaining. It is available as an app or physical timer (available in small and large sizes). Even without the bells and whistles, generic timers can work well for this purpose. We will revisit timers again as a tool to help in other Pillars.

"Itemize" your Regular & Routine activities.

Time becomes more relatable when you can draw a parallel between different activities that take the same amount of time to accomplish. Pay attention to how much time you spend on activities. Consider all the things you do, from getting up in the morning to the time it takes for you to get to your desk and set up for the day. A frequent blind spot is understanding just how much time is spent on things like showering and dressing, eating breakfast, prepping kids for school, walking the dog, traveling to/from school or work, checking email, etc. Perform this same review with work, school, or midday activities as well as evening routines.

Make a note of these consistent actions and what amount of time is typical for each—don't rely on memory. Organize them into tasks that take 15 minutes vs. those that take 30 minutes or even an hour. Then, as you schedule and plan your week, reference your itemized chart of activities. How much time truly remains after you correctly account for the time your regular activities already consume? Are you planning activities that you now see will take longer than the time you have available? You may find those 15-minute activities easily fit between meetings or are possible to do at the end of the day when you realize that they aren't as time-consuming as you once thought they were. It's typical to make a lot of adjustments in the beginning, but having this raised level of awareness and a timeframe upon which to base a starting point can move you further toward increased time awareness.

STEP 3
UTILIZE TIME TRACKING

Time tracking can feel like a burdensome exercise on the front end, but I've never met anyone who tried it that wasn't completely surprised by some of the findings. We can acknowledge that, at times, we all have a warped sense of how long activities truly take. This technique moves you from estimating to having the facts before you. Once you understand an activity you thought took 20 minutes takes upwards of 45, you improve your ability to be more realistic when planning. Try one of these:

Time Log. In its simplest form, this can be a list. Take time to quickly document all the activities you are doing and how long you spend on them. You can opt to make a list in an app or online document if you wish, but many people find it simplest to keep a designated sheet of paper handy to quickly jot down items. Tracking in real-time (as soon as you transition between tasks) can give the most accurate info but may feel cumbersome. You could also set a timer to ring every 30 or 60 minutes to remind you to stop and capture what you've done since your last update. Since activities can vary in the time needed, consider tracking your time with the time log over a period of a week or two so you see trends. Some activities will be predictable and consistent, while others may vary and span a range of time. Be sure to spend time at the end of the tracking phase to look at the data and see what jumps out at you. Where are you spending more time than you thought? Are there activities you do a lot more frequently than you thought? What tasks took less time than you anticipated? Where is there wasted time? What time of day did you get more done, and why may that have been the case? Several sample logs are included at the end of this chapter.

Online & technology-based trackers. If you cannot stomach the idea of manually logging your time, consider a tech-based tool that can assist, which will primarily help those who spend time on their computers as their primary workspace. These apps require setup time to be most efficient, as you need to define parameters of which tools and applications are productive for you and which may not be. For someone doing research, time spent on the Internet can be productive; for others, it may be a total time waste. Consider your role and if you can set guidelines to recognize where you are spending your time and flag it as beneficial vs. detrimental. For those tools and applications with a more complex setup, I err on the side of manual tracking as the most effective; however, if you know that won't happen, these tools can be a runner-up. A few to explore are RescueTime, Toggl Track, and HourStack. An online search can provide many options along with a comparison of their capabilities.

Work in set increments on ONE task. Frequent multitasking could be a culprit in hampering your time awareness. Managing many simultaneous activities used to be considered a positive skill, something we even bragged about or put on our resume as a strength. But we now know attention to our work often suffers while all tasks end up taking longer. To mentally shift between activities and get into a place of focus and creativity takes time. To begin to untangle those activities, better gauge how long they take, and focus more fully on the one thing before you, try working in set increments on that one thing:

- Use a timer
- Start small if you are just building your skills of single-focus. Set a timer for 20-30 minutes and focus solely on the task at hand.
- Eliminate distractions that may pull your attention elsewhere.
- When the timer goes off, assess your progress and determine if you want to set another 20-30 minute increment.

Practice this process of checking in as you move through the day to build mindfulness regarding the passage of time. You'll see which tasks require only one session and which need multiple rounds. You can decide to do each timed "chunk" one after the other or determine at the end of one task if you need revisit that work later or on another day based on your schedule. Remember, switching between tasks will require additional time to get back into the frame of mind and focus zone that is needed for the activity at hand.

Let me wrap up this step by adding that there *ARE* times when letting one activity get underway while you move on to another thing can work. Writing a quick email can be done while on hold or waiting for a Zoom meeting to begin. Listening to a podcast might allow some continuing education to occur while you handle some administrative filing or purging. The distinction is that these activities don't vie for your concentration or focus. Be selective in those things you choose to do simultaneously. If your Internal Time Clock is an area where you want to strengthen skills, it is still best to let multitasking take a back seat while you grow stronger in this area.

STEP 4

REFLECT

We often have so much going on that our instinct urges us to simply dive in and begin to tackle the work ahead that needs doing. To pause to reflect on a previous day or week might seem counterproductive as it delays you from jumping into action. Yet when you monitor your results, it gives great insight. What things took more time than you thought? Were there things you accomplished more quickly than expected? Did you plan too much to reasonably complete? If you blocked off time for a project, was it enough? How many things came up that you had to handle but didn't anticipate?

Reflecting is an important first step in planning and something I recommend for everyone. It is even more vital for those working to improve their time awareness. As you learn more and more about how things happened when compared to your intentions, you can become more and more equipped to understand how much time activities really take and can adjust your future planning to be more realistic. You may even find ways you can economize your time and cut down on time wasters!

Internal Time Clock
KEY TAKEAWAYS

Your internal time clock encompasses the ability to recognize, quantify, and calculate time. It considers how conscious you are of the passage of time in relation to the activities you are doing. It is about time awareness.

- How accurate is your internal clock? Can you usually home into where you are timewise in your day?
- Have new roles or regular multi-tasking impacted your ability to accurately gauge how long tasks take?

Set mile markers

- Building routines, using chimes, access to an outside view, and the use of notifiers can each strengthen your awareness of the passage of time.

Make the passage of Time relatable

- The use of analog clocks, timers, and regular, recurring activities can help us see and feel the passage of time

Time Tracking

- Time logs, whether paper or technology-based, help highlight the truth about how long activities take.
- Try working in set increments of time (10, 30, 60 min for example) to improve time awareness and track an activity's timing.

Reflect

- Regularly reflect on previous days to recognize where you are appropriately allotting time and where you may be over or under-planning the time needed for activities.

PILLAR 3
LONG-RANGE GOALS

WHAT DO YOU think of when you hear the word **Goal**? Does it inspire you, or do you feel intimidated? Have you identified a big dream you hope to achieve or have a big picture of the life you want to live? For some people, simply asking these questions will make their palms start to sweat! Some link the idea of goals to hard work, pressure, or struggle. Perhaps that's true when stretching to accomplish something new or difficult. Maybe the pressure to do or achieve feels overwhelming, not motivating.

I've worked with clients who know *what* they want to accomplish but don't know *how* to begin. Some have told me that they have a clear picture of the steps to take toward their goals but find it hard to make room for them alongside their daily responsibilities. Others have shared that they feel guilty or depressed at not having set big milestones or that they feel unmotivated or resentful of a goal that was imposed on them by someone else.

What would happen if you thoroughly explored what excites and motivates you? Could you let go of old goals, projects, or intentions that no longer serve you so that you have room to tap into your strengths and interests in new ways? Can you see a link between your day-to-day activities and your biggest priorities? What's missing, and where are you on target already?

If you can name your life goals right now, I congratulate you. It's a gift to have a clear view of where you are headed and what you want to accomplish. In truth, we all have goals, even if we haven't taken the time to label them fully or flesh out how to achieve them. Often, the "big picture" we have for our lives is made up of a variety of goals, and not all goals are alike. Some are short-term and very specific. Others are multi-layered and can span years. As we prepare to explore this Pillar and help you answer some of these questions, I'd like to introduce two different types of goals—**Finish Line** and **Lifestyle**. It may expand your view of what a goal can look like.

Finish Line Goals

These are goals that have a specific ending or outcome. They are often well-defined and can prove highly motivational. There will be a time when it is accomplished and the goal is complete. You'll cross the finish line and be done.

Examples of Finish Line Goals:

- Taking that trip to Alaska you've dreamed of
- Writing a book
- Getting that promotion
- Completing a degree
- Learning to play an instrument, or
- Finally cleaning out the attic

Conventional goal setting often lends itself to focusing on Finish Line goals exclusively. Breaking down a specific target, completing steps, and crossing it off your list. Yes, these are important, but to stop here limits your recognition of the more subtle yet powerful actions you can incorporate into your life. Let's explore a different type of goal.

Lifestyle Goals

Lifestyle Goals are targets for how you want to live life. They may be ongoing or perpetual. They may be about establishing boundaries in your life, creating "themes" or mantras to live by, and identifying things you wish to continue, add, or even remove from your life. Lifestyle Goals may flesh out how you wish to engage with others or perhaps your own individuality, gifts, and creativity. One person shared with me their goal of enjoying and continuing to live life as they are right now, as they were truly happy and wanted that to continue. I love that! I've talked with many individuals who have divulged that they "don't have any goals." Yet I find on further discussion that they do have things that they hold dear, intentions they want to pursue, and accomplishments they are aiming for. Lifestyle Goals could consist of aspirations such as:

- Spending more time with family
- Limiting time spent with toxic people or in negative environments
- Reading more/being a lifelong learner
- Maintaining a positive work environment with colleagues
- Focusing on their spiritual growth
- Volunteering regularly

Regardless of what your goals look like and the forms they take, they should come from a place that feels natural. While they may stretch you to grow, learn, and maybe even reach beyond your comfort zone, they shouldn't be in opposition to what feels instinctive. A life goal is internally driven. It should be based on where you are NOW in your life. When you find yourself connecting with things that excite you, that you enjoy, that you are good at, you can tap into a resource of energy that is like clean burning fuel—maximum output for a minimum of input and effort.

Within the Life Goals Pillar, we'll look at how your actions, roles, and routines align and support your life priorities and dreams. In other words, **"Do the things you spend time on move you closer to all you wish to accomplish?"**

Recognition of those things you are most passionate about, as well as understanding the work needed to act on them, makes this Pillar mighty. The power to be motivated and engaged comes from the seeds sown here. It supports your best productivity by focusing on your purpose, clarifying what's important, and carving a path toward reaching your objective. No other Pillar can make up for the weight supported here. Some find this Pillar challenging, especially if they've never taken the time to sincerely think about goals. For others, this Pillar may already be strong.

THE BENEFITS OF A STRONG GOALS PILLAR

It can feel as if goals sit above and outside of the day-to-day work to be productive. Yet they bring a critical component into the conversation. Clarity and strength in Life Goals fuel the very engine that powers our productivity. I see that as an asset in many ways.

You Know This Pillar is Strong If...
You have an Internalized sense of your "True North."

What makes a compass useful is that you can count on it to point north. It's a point of reference as you make your journey so you can chart a course and stay on track. Similarly, having a clear understanding of your objectives means knowing what you want to accomplish with personal, family, or career goals. It can clarify where you do—or don't—want to spend your time. Individuals strong in this Pillar have a good sense of where it's best to put their time and energy. The magnetic pull of their awareness keeps them on track.

You have a Consistency of Purpose.

In a world cluttered with information and options, it is easy to get mired down in all that goes on around us. Individuals with a strong sense of their Life Goals cut more easily through the extra noise of activity. Understanding where you want to be and what you set out to accomplish decreases the chance of being sidetracked by opportunities and activities that don't align with your ultimate goals.

Decision-making is simplified.

Clear objectives and goals act as a filter through which your decisions funnel. When provided with options or the need to choose between activities, strength in this Pillar can be a blessing. Rather than over-thinking where to invest your time and energy, there is clarity regarding which activities support you and which do not. That provides great peace of mind.

You have clarity on the "next steps."

Just as important as identifying your goals is knowing how to act on them. Strength in this area means the skills are there to break down and understand the next steps to get from where you are today to where you hope to be. Many people struggle with how to make that happen, so I celebrate those for whom this work happens more naturally. You can use this skill to tackle day-to-day activities as well as larger goals.

You experience motivation, energy, and contentment.

Being in tune with your true purpose is energizing. Think about how you can lose yourself in activities that you enjoy, are good at, or are motivated to do. The focus and exertion may seem minuscule compared to much simpler activities that don't resonate within us to the same degree. A strong Life Goals Pillar, where you understand what you are embarking on and are prepared to act, means operating on a plane of high satisfaction and purpose where the energy required to reach those goals is a renewable resource.

How Does *Your* Long-Range Goals Pillar Hold Up?

Do you relate to emotions or statements such as the ones below? If so, exploration and reinforcement of the Life Goals Pillar may prove beneficial:

- Exhibiting frustration, depression, low motivation involving activities, and use of time
- A feeling of being unproductive, unimportant, or unable
- "I never have time for..."
- "I don't know where to start!"
- "I don't know what to do now!"

While certainly not the *only* cause of these symptoms, a disconnect with Goals can manifest in these feelings. Frustration and sadness come into play when there is a sense of a bigger unknown out there that we feel we should move toward but cannot quite. Sometimes that is due to goals being unidentified or missing, so activities have no central purpose. A feeling of unimportance can emerge if we sense our daily lives aren't connecting to something larger.

Not tuning in to the *why* behind our actions can translate to a lack of motivation to get the work done. It can also feel highly unproductive when we don't know *how* to proceed. A lack of knowledge or training can stop us in our tracks before we even begin. We know we want to do something but may not know where to start, or the struggle may be in finding room in our days to move our goals forward. Since goals are so in line with our internal drive, it makes sense that not activating this area would lead to these emotions.

Let's move now to explore ways to address these struggles and move your Life Goals closer to reality!

MAKING YOUR GOALS A REALITY
TIPS & TECHNIQUES

Strengthening the Long-Range Goals Pillar begins with gaining clarity. We'll seek first to tap into your priorities, aspirations, dreams, and values. We want to move beyond those internal thoughts and intentions for "someday" to a place where you are ready to act "today." The tips and techniques offered here can help you define and select the goals that are most vital to you. Then the work continues as you identify the next steps and weave them into your day-to-day lives.

You may decide to dedicate a specific day or time to do a full Goal Setting Session, *or* you may add strategy and goal-building into a regular routine. Regardless of which approach you take, plan to revisit your Life Goals periodically. Life doesn't stand still, and neither should your goals.

If you feel you already have a clear understanding of your goals today, you can move ahead to Step Four, "Identify & Target." Feel free to skim the ideas in the pages that follow in case you wish to expand on what you already established as Life Goals or revisit this section for ideas you can use during a future goal-setting session. Let's move now to set the stage for the important and creative work that goes into defining your Life Goals.

STEP 1
SET THE STAGE

Capture your ideas.

You'll be generating many thoughts and ideas in the upcoming exercises. As you prepare, consider which technique would prove most helpful in capturing all that comes up during goal setting. There are many ways to get your goals, dreams, and aspirations out of your head and documented. It can be as simple as starting with pen and paper.

You may choose one of these simple techniques, or they may spark ideas for other methods you'd like to use.

Lists work well if you want to dive into many different ideas. Doing a "brain dump" to get everything bouncing around in your head out onto paper can help you assess what you already have in mind and free up space to generate new ideas or more fully flesh out those you already have. If you consider yourself a consummate list-maker, you can certainly employ it here!

Journaling works well if you wish to explore goals through more in-depth written dialogue. For some, the process of writing generates new ideas. It is a great medium if hands-on, tactile activity aids your focus and creativity. I've known clients who find the use of a favorite notebook, journal, or pen a way to honor the process and make it more special.

Whiteboards and flip charts allow you plenty of space to capture thoughts. You can stand back and observe what you are creating. Colorful Post-It notes can help if you want to move items around and capture thoughts in random order. Physically moving around the room as you work helps engage those kinesthetic processors. Similarly, taking time to walk or do other exercises might be a good start for those who feel the need to stay active or think well when in motion. Just be sure to capture those thoughts once you're done!

Mind mapping captures thoughts in a non-linear way. If brainstorming has you actively flowing between topics and introducing ideas as they crop up, mind mapping may be for you. The focus can be on a single project/goal, or you can use it to flesh out multiple ideas. As a theme/topic is added, related ideas, thoughts, or questions radiate outward, like a flow chart. For instance, if the goal theme is "Focus on my Health," ideas such as healthy eating, exercise, regular check-ups, family activities, or "things to avoid" could be possible branches from that central theme. Further reflection can then move within each of those areas while still allowing you to visually group your ideas. Mind maps can be written on plain paper, drawn out on a larger chart/board, or even done through a variety of applications that walk you through the process. This method engages both visual and tactile learners through the writing process as well as being able to see topics being fleshed out. Examples and free mind-mapping software can be found online if this is a new idea for you and you want to learn more.

Tap into your creative side. People have been greatly inspired when using vision boards. You can choose to take pictures, drawings, color, texture, words, or other materials to create a collage that represents your goals. Poetry, story-writing, and music can also be used to craft a creation that embodies your goals. The result should be a symbol of the destination you are aiming for. I've even employed lines of questioning that engage senses typically not used when thinking of goals, i.e., "If the coming year(s) was a blank wall, what would you write/draw on it?"

Talk it through. Some people use auditory techniques, processing thoughts and information best when they speak and hear it. Engaging a friend, colleague, or coach to walk through this exercise with you can be beneficial. It isn't about others helping you come up with your goals—rather, it's about creating a space to verbally digest your thoughts. A partner can ask questions to gain clarity or expand on your thinking. I've been with many clients who, as they are talking, realize they themselves have answered a question they've been asking for a while, or they've heard themselves clarify a thought or idea that they hadn't previously been able to fully grasp.

Find a creative and conducive environment.

I find that the right environment can greatly aid strategic thinking and goal setting. Think of a place that you find comfortable and motivating. What is it about that place that makes you feel that way? If it's

Pillar 3: Long-Range Goals

not possible to physically go there, are there components of this environment that you can incorporate where you are?

If you aren't sure what builds a productive environment for you, consider some of the things listed below. Some may resonate with you; others may not. These are to get you thinking about positioning yourself for high-level thinking and tapping into your goals. Consider your whole self as you goal-set—don't limit it to only your professional life. After all, you are one person, and your goals should be wholly reflective of you. If you did the work to tap into career aspirations but didn't move toward non-work dreams, you may still experience some of the frustration and lack of motivation mentioned earlier. How does each of these items impact you?

Sound: Do you need silence? Do you find music helpful? If so, what kind? Or do you prefer "white noise?"

Temperature: Are you hot or cold-natured? What temperature feels most comfortable so as not to be distracting?

Background Activity: Do you find that highly active places like coffee shops give you energy or prove distracting?

Sunlight vs. Artificial: If you feel the need to see daylight, working in a tucked-away conference room may prove draining. Get outside or find somewhere with lots of natural light if this is a mood lifter for you.

Workspace: What capture method will you use, and is there adequate space? Will you need a desk or table, or does a lot of wall space work best, along with room to move around freely?

Access to Information: What type of information will you need to access during your goal setting? Can it be at hand or available remotely if working away from your normal workspace?

Smell: Smells can prove highly distracting or extremely uplifting. They quickly tap into our emotions. If smell engages you, consider how to incorporate it. Some examples include candles, open windows, diffused oils, aromatherapy patches, and coffee or food.

Color: Could you place yourself in an area that activates you mentally through its use of color? Color Psychology and research on the impact color has on us is emerging and evolving. Some colors are invigorating, while others are calming. Some may be linked in our memories to events or can evoke mood and emotion. Even cultural uses of color vary. What colors could evoke your best environment for big-picture thinking?

STEP 2

BRAINSTORM

Once you've selected a technique to capture your thoughts and are in an environment that promotes creative thinking, you're ready to dive in! Brainstorming is an activity to generate and capture all your thoughts and ideas around a topic. At this point, don't worry about the steps involved, possible pros or cons, or even whether an idea is feasible or not—think outside the box here and allow even new and unexpected ideas to have a home. I ask clients to picture themselves dumping everything out of their brains and onto the table. You can work to sort, prioritize, select, and strategize later.

Some goals may be top-of-mind and bubbling to come out. I encourage you to get those captured first. That frees your mind for new ideas and deeper thinking to come. A series of questions and thought starters are provided below so you can continue your exploration. They are designed to help you build a description of a life, activities, and destinations to which you can aspire. Review the list and address those that jump out at you or get you thinking. If these don't inspire you, come up with some that do. The work now is to simply capture your thoughts. There is no wrong way to do that. Later steps will define what to *do* with what you've learned.

BRAINSTORMING YOUR GOALS
THOUGHT STARTERS

1. What are you doing when you are being your best self?
2. What are the various roles you serve? List your prime five to seven (you may group certain roles together). How/why are these important to you?
3. What activities build you up? Which activities weigh you down?
4. What do you want to spend more time doing?
5. What do you want to spend less time doing?
6. What are your favorite activities?
7. Where do you feel like you "waste" time?
8. Describe what you consider to be your biggest accomplishment. How did it impact you?
9. When you think of life as a journey, what do you consider your next destination?
10. In what areas of your life are you strong? Where and how is that strength exhibited?
11. Are there untapped areas of strength or talent inside you? What would it look like if you brought them out?
12. What is something you've always wanted to do, and why?
13. Imagine yourself on your 90th birthday reflecting on your life. What did it include? What didn't it include?
14. What one thing would you be most excited to see eliminated from your life?

15. What one thing would you be most excited to add to your life?
16. How does your professional life and/or involvement with groups or organizations support your personal priorities?
17. What is your greatest fear? Where does that fear compel you to do something you'd rather not do? Where does it hold you back?
18. What are things you feel you *should* only do because you see others around you doing them?
19. What tasks or areas of your life/career work well now? Define what makes it work well. How could you apply that in other areas of your life?
20. What tasks do you enjoy or find easy/natural? How could you do more of that?
21. What would you like to say "no" to so that you could say "yes" to something else?
22. Define what being "successful" means to you.
23. What does it mean to be successful in each of your primary roles?
24. Define what being "productive" means to you in your primary roles.
25. What activities make you *feel* most productive? Is this in line with your definition of productivity above?
26. Are there any areas where you feel you need permission to start or stop something?
27. If you could quit feeling guilty about something, what would it be?

> 28. What frustrates you?
> 29. What are you passionate about?
> 30. If you could pick a "theme" for the coming months, what would it be?
> 31. What is a dream you've always had?
> 32. If I were to look at my life as an outsider, what would I have questions about?
> 33. What other thoughts do you have about how you want to move forward?

STEP 3

EVALUATE

At this point, you may feel ready to get started on those goals. Or you may not be sure what to do next. Not to fear! This third step is an intentional pause. It's time to observe and evaluate what's there. Often, our instinct is to jump into action, but there may be things we miss in our haste. Take time to reflect on the words you've written, thoughts you've had, or conversations you've held as you passed through the brainstorming phase. There may be some specific pursuits you already know you want to accomplish, but you may also have some raw information resulting from the questions you answered. As you look at all you captured, ask yourself the following:

- What is it telling you?
- What have you learned?
- Were there any surprises?

- What recurring themes are there?
- How do you feel about what was uncovered?
- What's missing? Is there something you've held up as a goal only to find it didn't appear when you answered those questions? How does that make you feel?

Goal exploration and evaluation has been some of my favorite work with clients. When stepping back and looking at their responses, I've seen eyes get big as an answer or solution to a long-held question comes into focus. I've witnessed tears when realizations are made, seen peace come when there is clarity on a decision to be made, and heard excitement when realizing they held more self-knowledge and power than they'd given themselves credit for.

If you have never worked with a coach, this is an ideal time to partner with someone with the training to help you gain insight and dive deeper to explore those thoughts, perhaps challenge some long-held beliefs, and draw out goals that best resonate with you.

STEP 4

IDENTIFY & TARGET

Now you're ready to home in on specifics. You've gathered your ideas and evaluated them. *(Be sure that you've captured discussions and bigger notes, such as those done on a whiteboard or flip chart, so that you can reference these in the future.)* Next, it's time to identify goals you want to make a priority. Which ones will you target for *now*, and which will be for *later?* This step is where dreams and aspirations join with practical application. It's natural to be excited but also a little overwhelmed at this point. How can you begin to distill it all down so that you know where to start? This step helps you do just that!

How will you prioritize all you want to accomplish?

Is it a season where a focus on family takes precedence, or are there prospects in your work life that warrant some extra attention? Are there any timely opportunities that may not come again or to which you feel especially drawn? Maybe you'll choose to select one thing as a priority for each of the main roles in your life. Even if you don't have an answer right away, it's best to consider that **none of us can tackle everything we want to do at the same time.** You must be realistic to make those goals achievable.

What no longer belongs in your world?

As you begin to organize your goals, I suggest you approach it like you would a physical organizing project such as a closet, purse, or even a desk drawer. First, remove what doesn't belong, giving you room for what does. Assess everything you spend time doing now. Are there things you need to delete from your schedule? Do you need to jettison relationships or activities that prove toxic or unhelpful? Some changes may be easily within your control, such as rearranging your calendar and stopping certain activities. More self-control may be required to change routines and habits to avoid those things you've decided to eliminate. Others may involve more work, such as having difficult conversations, finding alternatives, tackling problems, or even addressing addictions. These can be daunting, and that may be why they've remained in your life.

What do you want to add to your life?

As mentioned at the beginning of this chapter, there are goals that have a defined completion, while others are ongoing. Goals may be something new you are setting out to do or achieve but could also include new things you wish to remain indefinitely. Examples of this could be building relationships with friends or family, adding health or spiritual practices to your life, etc. The table at the end of this section further breaks these down into things you want to increase/add to your life into a **sprint** (short term—taking only a week to a couple of months to accomplish) or a **marathon** (long term—taking greater than three months to accomplish). Again, refine the list further to distinguish between those you want to begin addressing now vs. later as well as which will be incorporated permanently or until the finish line is crossed.

You'll also see an area in the table to **capture those things you want to maintain**. It may seem strange not to focus solely on new projects and intentions when talking about goals. Here is why I find it important: There are ways we may be living our dreams right now. I've seen clients "overshoot" and feel discouraged that they hadn't set any goals. Their motivation was low, and they felt inadequate—as if they had been missing out. Then, on further reflection, we realize that they are already working toward or have achieved a life that makes them happy. There may still be some things they strive for, but what they hope to obtain isn't far off in the distance. When there has been that realization, it's mesmerizing to watch!

I still remember a client conversation I had years ago. James had a career goal to be a true representative or "face" of his law firm. He felt drawn to be a connector and highly active attorney. As he looked at his schedule, he saw a calendar full of not only his individual work but commitments his firm had asked him to make. He saw limited space to focus on his objective and felt quite discouraged. Then we started to look closely at the activities that were taking up his time. He began to see a correlation between the organizations in which he'd been asked to participate and the networking opportunities available at the events he attended. Where he had seen obligations that got in his way, he could now recognize prospects to achieve the very target he was aiming for. It was a huge paradigm shift for him, and I saw him light up with the thought that he wasn't so far away from his goals after all. Truthfully, nothing had changed in his schedule or with his goals. He simply saw and acknowledged something that was already happening. The motivation to participate in these outside meetings and events suddenly transformed from being a hindrance to being a path toward his Life Goal. It changed from draining him of energy to creating it.

What areas of your life would you benefit from acknowledging?

The table on the following page is designed to help you sort your actions and goals. Feel free to adapt this layout.

MY GOALS:

DATE: _____

	NOW	**LATER**
Things to Reduce/Remove:		
Things to Increase/Add:		
Finish Line Goals: Sprint: Marathon:		
Things I want to Maintain/Acknowledge:		

STEP 5

MAKE GOALS "ACTIONABLE"

A second component of this Pillar is determining *how* to set your goals in motion. Whereas the first part is focused on identifying and acknowledging the goal itself, the second is about making them actionable. We will look at how prepared you are to take the next step. Are you ready to bring the idea down from the conceptual level to "where the rubber hits the road?" Focus in this area is twofold: breaking down the goal into manageable parts so that it's clear what needs to happen *and* building a process to incorporate those steps into your day-to-day life so that the work brings it into reality.

A key to accomplishing your goals is to make sure they move from being **internal** to **external**. If the earlier exercises got you thinking about and pondering goals, but they're still only a reality in your mind, I encourage you again to get those goals, thoughts, and ideas out of your head and document them! Your first steps are to write them down, post them where you'll see them, and perhaps share them with others to build accountability. You can even tap into your creative side to fashion something that clearly represents the target of where your goals will take you. Could you use a picture or vision board to represent your goal? Do you enjoy journaling or find music as a good symbol for what you're working toward? I've found that once goals are external and documented or reflected in some way, analyzing the steps they will take becomes less daunting.

Some of your goals may already be very specific and tangible. Others may still be rather general or include a large goal with many components or layers. Consider the following as you work to break down larger, multi-step projects/goals. The more specific you make each step, the easier it will be to act.

- What are all the steps you need to take? Be as detailed as possible.
- What do you need to have at your disposal to take some of those steps?
- Where might you need to gain buy-in, funding, feedback, assistance, or even training?
- What are the milestones? What is the target for completion?
- Which ones may prove challenging? Which will be easy?

Once broken down and specific next steps are identified, next comes the proactive work to build time into your schedule for action. For those who claim to "know" what they want to do but "can't seem to get it done," this is often the missing piece. Review your schedule to determine if a set time works best to accomplish tasks that support your goals. You may have done this while creating your Schedule Model covered under the Planning Pillar—it's a tool to help formulate a plan and assign "homes" in your week for various activities. Or you may need to carve out different times on a week-by-week basis if a set time doesn't work for you or your typical schedule. Review your goals each week when doing your planning, and select a specific step(s) and a target day/time for when the goal will receive your attention and focus. There will likely be weeks when goals won't earn their way into your calendar, but if you regularly connect with them, over time, you'll have a process by which you don't lose sight of them.

This chapter has offered a lot of ideas that I hope will inspire you and provide ways to explore goals that are most meaningful for you. As a result, being motivated to get started is natural. An important consideration as you launch new initiatives is to find the right balance and be realistic. It's common to be full of motivation and enthusiasm. Consider what's reasonable given other things you have going on, your own abilities, and the "level of busy" that's right for you.

Finding that balance is a prime example of Time Management as a verb—the active work of considering all that you wish to accomplish, make choices about, and where to focus so that the right things get your attention and you don't burn out or lose momentum.

STEP 6
ANTICIPATE THE HURDLES

What hurdles may you encounter as you set out toward your goals? What might stop you in your tracks or slow down the process? I've seen momentum screech to a halt because something interfered with a goal moving smoothly onward. I remind my clients that they cannot be taken completely off guard if they see something coming down the road. Invest time to think through scenarios that might challenge you to begin, keep momentum, or complete that goal. That preparation equips you to act when—or if—it happens. When you recognize the roadblocks you may have to jump in order to accomplish your goal, you can proactively consider the action(s) needed to keep it going. Ask yourself:

- "What might happen to delay getting this done?"
- "Where do I need additional knowledge, input, training, etc.?"
- "What parts of this are challenging, unappealing, or unfamiliar?"
- "What could be done now that would decrease the likelihood of this hurdle impacting my progress?"

You likely won't need all the answers for *how* to get over your hurdles, but the hard work of anticipating and understanding them means you will be more likely to keep moving forward.

GOALS
KEY TAKEAWAYS

Goals reflect the direction and design you envision for your life. The work within this pillar also aims to translate your high-level, big picturing thinking down into actionable steps.

Building Awareness:

- What techniques work best for you when capturing your thoughts and intentions toward goals?
- How can you Set the Stage and build an environment for work and focus that is most effective?
- Did the Brainstorming exercise bring up any new realizations for you?

Evaluation:

- Did any themes emerge as you considered your goals? Are there any goals you need to add or leave behind?

Identification:

- What are your Finish Line Goals and/or your Lifestyle Goals? Which take priority and need your attention now vs. later?

Making Goals "Actionable:

- Have you captured your goals "externally" vs. just in your head? *You can use the worksheet shared earlier in this chapter.*
- Which goals need to be broken down to identify the steps necessary?
- How can you keep your goals close at hand so that they are available when you plan your days and weeks?

PILLAR 4
LEVERAGE: HABITS & BEHAVIORS

WE'VE ALL HAD days that begin with a well-thought-out and realistic plan but end up going "to hell in a handbasket!" Do you feel plagued by last-minute requests or constant interruptions? Maybe distractions, unexpected changes, and shuffling schedules keep you from working your plan. Still, other culprits are sneakier and hard to pinpoint. Could the need for perfection lead you to spend too much time on some things or delay until you have all the info you'll need? Is there more on your plate than you'd like because you have reservations about handing it off to others or feel it will take longer to train someone else than simply doing it yourself? After all, things might not get done the way you'd like.

Even with a practical plan for your day in hand, these examples show that more is needed to stay productive and on target. You can't always change what comes at you from the outside. But you CAN fine-tune and improve how you respond and react. This Pillar addresses the behaviors that help you monitor and control your own actions and attention. Where planning is deciding where time will be best spent, **this Pillar is about the self-discipline to follow through on those actions you've determined are most essential. It's about FOCUS.** Society and technology often work against us. We have more information and communications than ever before coming at us in a constant stream. Proficiency here helps you **spend more time on high-value items and less time on minutiae and distractions.**

Harnessing the power of habit is a key technique within this Pillar. Simply put, a habit is a pattern of behavior that has become predictable and routine. A large portion of our actions each day stems from habits: mannerisms, motions, activities, reactions, thoughts, etc. Once learned and ingrained, habits don't require much mental energy to prompt them to happen. Think about brushing your teeth or putting on your seat belt when in the car. It feels strange when you DON'T do these things, yet you probably don't have to will yourself to do them. The action becomes routine, and you don't think about it—you just do it. The brain work behind it no longer resides in the prefrontal cortex, where active and conscious decision-making occurs; it is moved into the basal ganglia, at the core of our brain, which stores memory and pattern recognition. When you build good habits, not only do you reap positive results, but you also reserve mental energy, which you can spend on other things.

Yet, as handy as habits can be, there are times when they prove problematic. That's because a habit's job is to make your world/life/mood better NOW without considering the long-term effects. So, habits may exist that hamper the very things you hope to achieve. If churning through email provides a sense of distraction from less engaging or difficult tasks or gives you a feeling of productivity through "busyness" (remember rabbit hole productivity mentioned earlier?), you may see that habit creep in when you really should be focusing on an important upcoming deliverable or task. As you evaluate your patterns, it's good to consider any unhelpful habits you may have picked up. Do they lead to avoidance or relieve stress? What activities have become "comfort food" for your time? They make you feel better in the moment but aren't necessarily healthy. We can't unlearn a habit, but you can overlay it with better ones when you tie a new activity to more appealing and productive outcomes. Where can you make different choices linked to healthier results?

The Leverage Pillar includes the ways we operate and manage ourselves on a day-to-day basis. How effective are you at maintaining focus and concentration, making decisions, managing procrastination or perfectionism, prioritizing high-value activities, and mitigating distractions, to name a few? Other proficiencies also fall into this area that may not have traditionally been considered time management skills: effective communication, conflict resolution, or acknowledging fear or doubt and how it impacts your actions.

This is the broadest of the 6 Pillars in that it encompasses a wide array of topics. Included in this section are tips and techniques for issues that I see most frequently with clients and organizations. However, this isn't inclusive of *every* possible skill that can reside in this area. You may even recognize some of these skills as strengths you possess while others are things you'd like to improve. Consider which ones impact you most. While most of us can benefit from a tune-up on many habits or behaviors, you can see the biggest impact when selecting one or two to approach first.

THE BENEFITS OF A STRONG LEVERAGE PILLAR

Strength in this area shows up when an individual can stay engaged and active throughout the day. These are the people gifted with the power of **action**. There are so many variables at play around your habits and self-management. Strength in this area equips you to mitigate the minefield of distractions, stay focused, curb perfectionism, tackle procrastination, and improve decision-making. Even when things sneak into your day to throw you off course, skills within this pillar can help you recover and get back on track. It can smooth the road to better navigate your day and put your plan into motion more easily.

You Know This Pillar is Strong If...

You are ready to aim, fire, and GO!

When teamed with effective planning, those with strong self-management skills can accelerate their productivity like no one else! You're less likely to get mired down by bad habits and succumb to lesser priorities. Armed with a purposeful plan and motivation, you can get into the productivity zone right out of the gate.

You capitalize on good habits.

Those strong in this area recognize the power of focus. Armed with experience, you see and feel the positive results when you look beyond the distractions "in the moment" and aim for the end goal—completing high-value activities. The key to developing good habits is linking a certain behavior to a beneficial outcome so that repeating that action yields positive results. Good habit formation and self-discipline beget more of the same.

You have fewer things blocking "activation."

Newton's Law of Motion begins with "An object at rest stays at rest, and an object in motion stays in motion." There is a momentum that transitions you from being *at rest* to being *in motion*, which I refer to as **activation**. In my work with clients through the years, there have been many conversations over the puzzle of why a person fails to begin—or activate—when the task at hand is clear and manageable. I believe part of it ties to the fact that a greater amount of energy is required when you first engage in an activity. Those who regularly exercise good discipline regarding their time use are already "bodies in motion." Moving from task to task takes less energy.

You spend less time thinking—more time doing.

As mentioned earlier, those strong in this area have the power of action on their side. I see a tendency in these individuals to take the first steps without unnecessary hesitation or delay. This tendency shouldn't be confused with jumping ahead before good decisions can be made, or the requisite information is gathered. Rather, this strength is the ability to eliminate the pause that often happens when you should be starting. "Should I do more research?" "Is it OK to proceed?" "If I can't finish today, should I even start?" Those questions may still be on the table, but someone proficient in this Pillar won't let it stall the process.

How Does *Your* Leverage Pillar Hold Up?

There is a broad range of skills that fall within this Pillar. It is worth looking more deeply at this area when symptoms such as these are exhibited:

- Difficulty staying on task
- Easily distracted
- Waiting till the last minute because "I work better under pressure."
- Addiction to communication and social media
- Addressing things as they pop up vs. at an appropriate time
- Procrastination, perfectionism, lack of delegation

The common denominator for the symptoms in this area is that each can hijack your day. Some are initiated by outside sources, such as interruptions by others, noisy environments, pop-up notifications, or when someone supersedes your plan with a new or more pressing request. Others can crop up without outside influence. The problem may lie in a struggle to stay focused. Regardless of the catalyst, the root skills to mitigate them are *internal*.

When I hear from a client that they regularly get pulled away from the task at hand, it cues me to look not only for the cause but also to explore their ability to navigate those interruptions and get back on track. Do you get derailed only by distractions from others, or do you struggle to focus even when uninterrupted? References to working better under pressure, frequent procrastination, or difficulty concentrating may signal problems with self-management. Attention is easily diverted by thoughts, diminished attention span, or struggles to prioritize.

The symptoms that show up around this Pillar—your habits and self-management—are those things that occur "outside the plan." Hints that this Pillar may need attention stem from what happens throughout your day. Looking back over the day or week to see where your *reality* deviated from your *intention* starts to shed light on what is really going on. No one (at least that I know) plans to procrastinate, spend too much time on email, or take far too long to make something "perfect." Interruptions may be a way of life, but you should also reflect on how well you can transition back into critical thinking once returning to the original task. What cropped up that wrestled the steering wheel from your hands and began to drive your day? How did your action—or inaction—divert you from the original plan for your time? When you don't fully understand what is at the heart of your self-management difficulties, the assumption may be that you are simply a poor time manager and often "your own worst enemy." Self-defeat, guilt, and frustration can be the emotional side effects of these symptoms.

The good news when considering all these internal skills is that they can operate independently. Having deficits in this area doesn't mean that all components are weak. I'd venture to say that even those who end up being relatively strong in this Pillar likely have one or two of these skills that they could improve. Look back at the questions shared at the beginning of this section—did you see anything that looked familiar or hit especially close to home? Reflect on which red flags show up for you more regularly than you would like. Recognize that those things that live within your control are those over which you can have the biggest impact. It can be hard work to get to the root issues, and it takes ongoing practice to change behaviors, but the power lies within YOU—and that's empowering.

LEVERAGING YOUR HABITS & BEHAVIORS
TIPS & TECHNIQUES

Within this Pillar, we'll walk through many of the topics you typically see in time management articles, podcasts—you name it. That's because they do have a big impact. They help you build focus and limit the pull of time wasters and inefficiencies. Review them all but focus on a few. You may wish to make small tweaks to some areas and be more diligent with implementing multiple techniques provided for those you want to improve most. Feel free to add your own touches and methods for what makes each work for YOU.

To simplify the many topics within this Pillar, they are grouped into six key steps:

1. Internal Dialog—identify ways your mindset, emotions, etc., can impact productivity
2. Build Habits—create routines and actions that streamline your effectiveness
3. Work the Plan—incorporate your plan throughout the day and week
4. Tips to "Get Going"—prioritize, activate, and maintain your focus throughout the day
5. Stop What's Stopping You—keep distractions, perfectionism, and procrastination in check
6. Optimize your Interactions with others—delegate and communicate effectively

You may find that other issues come to mind that impact you in this area but are not covered here. These techniques address the most common indicators I see in my work with clients.

Before beginning, remember that we are each differently abled. At the beginning of this book, I noted ADHD and other brain-based challenges as influences towards the overall approach to Time Management and traditional organizational techniques. I still hold firm that the 6 Pillars are each relevant, regardless of your capabilities or neurodiversity. We all need to implement strategies that work best for ourselves, according to our abilities.

Brain-based conditions often impact this Pillar most directly. The brain's executive function is highly active as we motor through our days. Activities of attention management, distractions, prioritization, interruptions, handling challenges, etc., draw on our capacity continually. Brain-based conditions span a wide range of issues and can show up differently for every individual. As you review the topics in this section, weigh these tips and techniques alongside what you know to be true about yourself. Consider your capabilities and how they influence your use of time.

STEP 1
LISTEN FOR INTERNAL DIALOG

Emotion is one of the first filters through which we process our thoughts. It makes sense to acknowledge that our actions and reactions are flavored by how we feel about an activity and the internal dialog going on inside us. I bring this topic up first because it can be an underlying issue that results in some of the topics and symptoms we cover later. If you have fears or self-doubt, it can lead to trepidation, perfectionism, or avoidance. Past experiences might impact your willingness to delegate, cause you to struggle with procrastination, or influence how you interact with others. Mindset can head you down a positive or negative path, and your level of confidence impacts how you set out to address a task. Certainly, not every bit of inefficiency is seeded in some emotional difficulty, but it is helpful to see where there are trends. When you increase your self-awareness, you equip yourself to get to the root of problems more accurately regarding habits and self-management.

A simple step to improve that awareness is taking time for regular reflection. I suggest building this practice into weekly planning. It can feel counter-intuitive to our busy lives, which are often focused on "what's coming next," but incorporating a look back at the previous week(s) for signs where internal dialog may have been at play can be helpful. It builds a habit of learning from past actions and allowing what you find to raise awareness as you head into the week ahead.

Following are some questions to consider as you weigh where internal dialog may be taking the reins and impacting your day-to-day productivity. Not all may speak to you, but is there one that gives you pause? Consider their impact in the past but also recognize where it could pose a hurdle going forward.

Explore your Internal Dialog.

As you plan for the week ahead or review the prior week, use these questions for exploration:

- Can you see where your attitude or mindset impacts the actions you take or avoid?

- Is fear at play? How strong is that fear? Is it based on something you *know* or something you *assume*? If that fear plays out, what's at stake?

- Where might you be overestimating? Where might you be underestimating? This could be regarding yourself, others, the expected outcome, the difficulty of the task, etc.

- What's behind your hesitation? Is it something you need to understand more fully before you take action? Is there information you need to receive? Is it knowledge or training you need to gain? Is it based in fear?

- Is there a disconnect between your goals and the activities on which you spend your time?

- What is your first reaction when looking at a task or activity?

- Are there places where your relationship with another person (good or bad) alters the way you address an activity?

In summary, you're looking for the strong emotional reactions at play. What thoughts or words enter your mind? Is there a message there for you to hear and understand? Does it shed light on how you act or react?

Get creative.

For more creative exploration, assign a different color for activities you are excited about, those you have neutral feelings toward, any that feel troublesome or problematic, or those you simply dislike. Feel free to divide up your categories differently if you wish. You may even choose to select types of music, textures, numbers, or emojis instead of color—use what speaks to you.

Now, using your categories, look at the activities from last week or the week ahead. Which ones jump out? Can you see where any habits crop up in conjunction with the category you assigned? This reflection isn't about judging ourselves, only about awareness. What does that knowledge arm you with so you can improve your Habits and Self-Management?

STEP 2

BUILD HABITS FOR THE WIN!

You can enlist the wonderfully compact and efficient tool that is a habit to improve your skills involving productivity. By capitalizing on your brain's natural tendency to remember and file habits, you can automate to some degree those activities you deem to be valuable and routine.

Habit development boils down to identifying a precise activity, experiencing the positive results from it, and cementing the two together through repetition. Once these actions evolve into habitual behaviors, there is less mental energy needed to initiate them, and their regular occurrence is instinctive. So, on to the tips to build strong, helpful habits:

Identify the habit being built.

Is there a *specific* behavior or action you want to make routine? Be sure the definition is clear. The habit may be something you want to **start doing** (like planning weekly, a daily routine, exercise, industry reading, game night with your family, etc.), but it could also be about **something you want to avoid or stop doing** (like checking email first thing each day, staying up too late, too much time on social media, etc.) What exactly do you want to happen because of this new habit?

Be internally motivated.

Setting out to build a new habit requires commitment. There is a higher degree of success when the reason and value of the activity genuinely resonate with you. If you're drawn to initiate a new routine or habit because it is a "good idea" or someone you know does it, there likely won't be the staying power of something that is driven by your own priorities and goals.

State the specific action(s) you will take.

Even if the goal is avoidance of another activity, you need to define specifics regarding what you will *do* in its place to create the new habit. Here are a few examples:

What are the criteria? This is the who, what, when, where, and how. Give yourself some specific ways to put the habit in motion.

What is the frequency required? Habits require repetition. Like wearing a path in the grass over time, a habit requires that you tread the route frequently. After the first pass, the grass will spring back to its original state, but over repeated, frequent passes, a clear route begins to form. Will you aim for a daily habit, multiple times a week, or less frequently? There are no guarantees about how long it takes to develop a habit. Your motivations absolutely play a part but cannot serve the same role as a regularly repeated action.

Keep it front-of-mind until autopilot takes over. Consider how children learn to brush their teeth. It starts as a daily routine where someone older does it for them. Then, the child does it themself with someone monitoring and coaching as needed. That evolves to the child being given only a reminder to brush their teeth and, eventually, no prompt is needed at all. As adults, what prompts and reminders could best support you when new habits aren't yet part of your instinctive actions? This is a point where many people fall off the habit-forming bandwagon. They get excited to start a new, positive routine but simply lose sight of them as they get wrapped up in their former routine. Creating these reminders can be a fun and creative activity. Think about your own style—what could make this new designated activity jump out and get your attention? What can help build accountability and keep you on track? The next page contains a few ideas to get your creative juices flowing:

BUILD THOSE HABITS!

- **Give yourself Signs and Visual Cues.** Whether it's bright post-it notes to yourself, a picture, a pop-up reminder, or something new in your environment (I.e., flowers, a new planner, a candle, etc.), the goal is to visually remind yourself of your intention.
- **Find an Accountability Partner.** There is great power in expressing an intention to another person. Is there someone that can check in with you on your progress? Can you self-report to a colleague, family member, or coach?
- **Assign the activity a regular time in your calendar.** Treat the activity like an appointment and block time specifically for that activity. This scheduling is especially helpful for habits with less frequency than daily since the longer we go between occurrences, the easier it is to forget. You may want to set an alarm as a reminder if it isn't something you will easily remember.
- **Build in rewards.** Can you postpone something you enjoy until you've completed the habit-building activity? Or, can you select a perk you'll allow yourself as an acknowledgment that you stuck with it? Make it something that you truly see as a reward and not something you will do anyway, regardless of completing your habit activity.
- **Clear the way.** Are there steps you can take ahead of time to make it easier to do the activity when the time comes? That could be laying out your workout clothes before bed so you can more easily prepare for the alarm and early-morning jog or weekly meal-planning so that you're less likely to choose fast food after a busy day. It can also be preparing the information and materials so that you have everything ready to go and visible when you sit down to work in the morning instead of resorting to email while you decide what you're going to tackle. Look at what often

> stops you from acting to find clues on where you'd benefit from clearing the way.
> - **What has worked for you in the past?** There's nothing like drawing on your own experiences and preferences when deciding what may work best for you. Think about how you can effectively keep the new routine going until the habit becomes automatic.

STEP 3

WORK THE PLAN

We covered planning earlier, but **simply having a plan isn't what keeps you on track**. Like a boat that drifts in the current, your attention can drift on the daily barrage of incoming emails, projects, urgencies, and interactions if you don't have a way to stay focused on your intentions. To avoid drifting, **limit the places you need to look for "what's next."** Build the habit of working your plan to anchor your focus.

The first Pillar addressed how to identify the best structure for your time and decide where to put your focus for the week ahead. It concentrated on the *activity* of regular planning; the act of *working* that plan resides here, within "Pillar 5—Leveraging your Habits & Behaviors." Staying on track with your plan involves self-management throughout the day. **Your plan can serve as the single most valuable source of direction for your day** when you regularly follow these steps:

1. **Review.** When you create your plan at a weekly level, you don't need to go back to the drawing board every morning. This review is planning's daily component—looking at the plan you created to identify whether any adjustments are needed. What didn't get done yesterday

and needs to move forward to today, later this week, or be rescheduled for a future week? What does your calendar hold? What are your priorities for the day? Has anything come up to change those priorities? Before you get drawn into other things, look closely at the intentions you set when you planned your week.

2. **Navigate.** Don't "set it and forget it." Reference your plan periodically throughout the day. It serves as a reference point to keep you on track and to flag you when adjustments are needed. Our days are dynamic—schedules change, and priorities shift. Navigation involves all those tiny "course corrections" we do throughout the day. Where might things need to be moved on your calendar? When something gets added, will another activity need to be shifted, making room for it? What's been completed? What remains? If you connect with your plan regularly, you have a tool that will help you adjust as needed but still stay focused on your ultimate priorities.

3. **Funnel your activities.** Tasks and to-dos come at us from multiple sources, and it's hard to keep track of all that needs to get done. Does email generate follow-up work and meeting requests? Do you use a client or project management tool that generates work? Do you keep hand-written lists and reminders? Maybe others in your world generate work and responsibilities for you—whether personal or professional? Where possible, funnel incoming tasks or block time to work on specific activities into your planning system as they come up. If it's too cumbersome to transfer ALL tasks into one single planning tool or list, at least narrow down

the places you have to look for direction, which will help your plan remain the most comprehensive guide to where your focus should be aimed. Capturing and managing tasks will be covered in more detail later in "Pillar 6—Resources & Tools."

4. **Close out**. At the end of the day (or as a starting point for the following day), reflect on the outcome of the day/week with the following in mind:

How did the day/week flow? Think about the structure of your days and where activities landed. Given your schedule, was the number of tasks you planned appropriate? Are there ways that you can adjust your schedule and your plan so it can be more effective?

Where were the successes and challenges? Were you able to maintain focus, or did you get pulled off course? Did an urgency or a request by someone else impact your day? Where did things run smoothly? What was the best part of the day and why?

What remains undone or unfinished? This assessment is not about judgment—it's the practical work of deciding what to do with the incomplete items so that they are not overlooked. Is there time available in the coming day(s) to work them in? Do other priorities mean that this needs to be set aside until a future week?

Move things forward so that there is no need to look back. You can't fully rely on a plan if you have the nagging feeling that you've overlooked tasks on yesterday's list. Closing out the day means you move forward any items left undone. Adjust due dates, move tasks or next steps to a future day, or make notes to revisit it during planning and get it rescheduled. It is reassuring to know that your plan for today is about today only and that everything behind you has been closed out through completion or adjusting the target date to tackle it.

So ... What happens when the best-laid plan goes out the window? Regardless of our skill at planning, things come up to change those plans. I've come to realize that a close second to skillful planning is being adept at making modifications when life throws you a curve ball. If you tend to throw in the towel when your schedule or tasks get shifted, then you turn over control of your focus and activities to external factors. Think about how you react when your plan for the day starts to veer away from what was intended. Do even small changes shift your mindset? Do you find it easy to get back on track? What's the source of those changes? Are they within your control, or does it speak to the responsiveness of your position? Most days don't turn out exactly as we foresee them. **Many people consider their time management a success only when their actions for the day exactly match the plan. But is that a realistic expectation?** Sure, it's nice when you have a day when all goes according to schedule and you accomplish all you set out to do initially. Our planning certainly targets that objective. Yet I think it glosses over the reality of most days. If you struggle to recoup after a big change of plans, try these steps to reassess and regain awareness and decision-making regarding your time:

1. **Take a deep breath.** Really. Deep breathing helps us shift from our "reactive brain" and reengage our "thinking brain." Three deep breaths prove helpful in putting us back into the most productive frame of mind.

2. **Assess how much impact the change will take.** Does the change of plans add anything to your schedule? Does it add or change the tasks you'll be able to address? Does it do both? Look not only at the current day but the remainder of the week for which you planned. Is

something being added or removed? What is the container of time that will remain, given the change?

3. **Look at what needs to shift in your plan.** Too often, a change makes us go back to the beginning and reconsider everything we need to do. Instead, look at the plan itself. Since this is a narrower list of tasks and scheduled activities, first examine those to determine what needs to change. Can any of your tasks be moved ahead to another day, or can you reschedule them when you plan next week? Where might you need to enlist help? What are your options?

4. **Take proactive steps to notify others of changes and reset expectations.** Before you begin to panic over a looming deadline or meeting, consider reaching out to the people who may be impacted. While you may not be able to shift or postpone all your commitments, you can at least open communication about your impacted availability. You may even find that others are open to adjusting those expectations or appointments.

5. **Boil it down—what can remain in this week's plan, and what needs to be set aside?** When you have a plan in place, you may still need to make changes, but there will be fewer pieces to move.

STEP 4

GET GOING!

This step incorporates the skills that help you get started and keep your "eyes on the prize." Sharpening these skills not only GETS you going but KEEPS you going!

Prioritize and Make Decisions.

Being proactive and intentional with your time rarely happens by accident. Without the ability to prioritize, you fall susceptible to the temptation to address things simply as they come up or based solely on urgency rather than through consideration of their level of importance and value. It takes self-discipline to rise above someone else's crisis or to resist those things that catch your eye on top of the pile or email inbox. In fact, the whole of Time Management is the sum of making effective decisions + staying focused on them.

The process of decision-making first came up in "Pillar 1: Planning" and again in "Pillar 3—Goals." Within those Pillars, you make decisions as you look at your projects/priorities and then strategically plan time for activities to support those goals. Where it comes into play within this Pillar is with all the ways you make decisions throughout your days. You constantly filter options and make choices as you navigate:

Your daily tasks. Which ones stand out as the highest in importance? How do you determine which moves to the front of the queue?

Changes that come up. How do you shuffle your activities and priorities when something happens to shift your original calendar or plan?

New opportunities. When new ideas, projects, and conversations bring new possibilities, how do you fold them into your current plan?

The way you make decisions and then prioritize them has many components, processed at lightning speed. It's a balancing act between many factors. So, what drives your decisions? Below are a few reasons I see my clients often decide to do—or not do—an activity:

- Deadlines and urgencies
- Who is asking? (Boss, family, people we like, people we don't)

- Area of responsibility (Should you be doing it, or someone else?)
- Timing (Is something making *NOW* the right time to take something on?)
- It's important to you (It supports a goal, has high value, you enjoy doing it, etc.)
- Provides opportunities (Can taking this on lead to new, positive things?)
- Avoidance (is it something you dread, find boring, don't understand, etc.?)
- How they're feeling (How you feel physically or emotionally might impact your willingness to take on the task *now*.)

Within the word *priority* itself is "prior"—something that comes first. Not only must you decide what you'll act on, but you also weigh which tasks and actions deserve to be put before others. Which factors weigh heaviest may even change weekly. Some people like to have deadlines, and the timing of those deliverables takes precedence. Others need to prioritize based on what the boss has asked them to do. Still, others may choose to capitalize on a new opportunity or focus on their long-range goals. Pay attention to those things that get bumped down the priority ladder as a means to avoid doing it. Do you wait until they're on fire before you tackle them?

Once you make decisions and identify which activities are most important, make them visible and recognizable for what they are—priorities. You have a greater chance of successfully completing them when you take steps to flag them as significant. Some simple techniques to acknowledge those priorities are:

- Highlight them, circle them, or note them in a different color.
- Put them at the top of your task list OR schedule a specific time for priority activities.
- Tackle them first—if priorities get your time at the start of the day, there is less chance other activities will push them aside or crowd them out of your day.
- Write a very specific action(s) to take. The more detailed you make your task or next step, the less chance you'll procrastinate.
- Use the note-card technique. A colleague of mine would put her task list on an index card. The front contained only her 1-3 priority tasks. Other tasks were on the back. She could only flip to the back side once the priorities were complete.

Come up with your own creative way to make priorities the "headliner"!

Activate.

Remember—*Activation* refers to that initial burst of energy it takes to set yourself in motion. You need to activate when you begin your day, start a project, get back to work after a break or interruption, and even when you change gears and move from one task to the next. A failure to activate might signal the onset of procrastination, a bigger issue we'll cover in the next step, but I've come to recognize that this component can be a sticking point in itself. I've seen problems with activation occur with seemingly benign tasks and even those that are eagerly anticipated. Clients have had next steps defined, and there was plenty of intention and willpower to start, but something seemed to hold them back. It proves frustrating to those who struggle with it because they don't understand their hesitation or failure to simply "do it."

A pause seems to occur when our mind sees upcoming tasks and immediately applies filters to strain out activities where there's any argument for NOT beginning. It can result in attention and work only being given to those tasks that are highly engaging and interesting OR those that absolutely must be done to avoid a significant, negative consequence. If you struggle to activate, here are a few tips to help:

Stay "in motion." The effort it takes to begin any activity from a standstill is greater than what is required when we are already in an active state. For times when you struggle to activate on tasks, place them throughout your day when you are in transition between activities and already have momentum. That can mean you take advantage of the 15 minutes between appointments to address an email you've been meaning to send, use the time while your coffee brews to address the clutter of mail that tends to pile up, or start the first step on an important project before you have time to do anything else in the morning. Capitalize on the times when you are already physically and mentally active.

Say it out loud. "I am going to _____" is a simple statement that is decisive and focused on action. When you verbalize a statement of intent, it no longer resides solely in your head. Whether you speak to yourself, a family member, or a colleague, keep the statement specific to the exact action you will do and by when. Mastermind groups and accountability partners are common places where this is put into practice. As you make statements to others, it helps formulate the plan into specific steps with timeframes for completion. When feeling "stuck," putting it out there for others to hear can be a key motivator to move it forward!

Focus on beginning, not finishing. Activation stalls if there is concern that the task can't be fully completed in time. It feels too big to do *now*. That is especially true if the work you are to begin involves multiple steps or your perception of how long the action will take is inflated. Aim to start. Worry about finishing later once the work is underway. You may surprise yourself and check the list off altogether, but even if that's not the case, you'll have made headway, and continuing on can be less onerous.

Beat the clock. This is a way to promote action and focus your brain on the time limit rather than on ways to talk yourself out of beginning. I especially like the use of timers or stopwatches, but anything from hold times, waiting for the kettle to boil, or the commercial breaks during a program can serve the same purpose. Another option is to assign an "action hour" at the best time of day for your energy level and funnel those things you struggle to activate on into that container of time. Can you make it a game to check off as many items on your list as possible? How far can you get before time is up?

Build your Focus and Concentration.

Once activated, the next layer is to build concentration skills so you can maintain focus, attention, and energy toward the work at hand. That's a skill that proves difficult for some and can be a real challenge in our world today. Does your mind easily wander, or do you regularly struggle to manage disruptive thoughts and internal distractions? Maybe you're susceptible to hyper-focusing and get so absorbed in an activity that all other things are tuned out. Both present their own challenges, as they can derail your plans. If you find you frequently struggle with focus, review the techniques below:

Understand what's reasonable. There is a natural cycle to concentration. Even those who focus easily will max out at about 45-90 minutes tops before their productivity and attention span starts to wane. If your role warrants long periods of focus and concentration, consider ways to work with that rhythm, maximize focus, build in breaks, and transition back into focus time. Targeting a full morning of non-stop concentration overshoots that natural rhythm for most people and can prove de-motivating rather than helpful if you can't hold your focus for that stretch of time. Instead, break up long stretches of focus work time into smaller components or "cycles." You can aim for two or three cycles of concentration vs. one long stretch. If your role is dynamic and requires you to shift attention frequently, your ability to concentrate may be harnessed best in 15-30 minute "sprints." Consider what works best for you and your time requirements throughout the day, and set that as your target.

Start small and grow gradually. To build your skills focus and attention skills, start with a small amount of time. Set a practice goal—perhaps 10-15 minutes. Choose a task on which you will work solely during that stretch. Pick an activity that is manageable but not too easy. Most of us don't find it hard to engage in things that are our favorite activities, so give yourself a bit of a challenge here. Set a timer. When time is up, consider what that amount of time felt like. Was it hard to concentrate? Did your mind wander? Did you get "fidgety" or struggle to stay physically still? Were there interruptions? What changes could you make to be more successful at concentrating? If it was challenging, determine if you want to aim for that same amount of focus time or if you may need a shorter interval while you work to build proficiency. Reset the timer and begin again. Like any skill, focus takes practice. If you haven't actively worked on that ability, don't be surprised if it takes some time to stay on-task. When you begin to get comfortable with these stretches of concentration, gradually lengthen each interval or link together two or three shorter segments. Some are able to build their stamina and focus until they can work for 45 minutes or longer, then take a short break to stretch or take a mental pause before returning to work. The goal is to regularly build in time for focusing so that the capability is there when you need it.

Tackle hyper-focusing. You may have the opposite challenge than the one we just covered— you get involved in something and lose all track of time. Utilize an external prompt or alarm to pull you back to awareness after a designated span of time has passed. Timers or alarms on your computer, watch, or phone can be set to provide an audible notifier that it is time to "come up for air." At that point, you can determine if it is time to move on to other tasks on your plan OR choose to continue. More details are covered in "Pillar 2—Internal Time Clock," which can help you address this issue.

Utilize "cues" to signal focused work sessions. The idea behind this technique is to utilize something unique in your surroundings when you are concentrating on a specific activity. For instance, light a candle when you begin to study, turn on a specific genre of music when writing, etc. The cue becomes a constant signal linked to a specific action. Over time, the cue becomes a trigger, helping you transition into a place of attention and focus more quickly and easily. You can expand on this method with one of the ideas below or conceive one of your own to create the most effective "cues" for your focus time:

- Designate a place/work area (table, seat, room, etc.) to be used specifically for one type of task or activity.
- Select a single, visible item such as a candle, picture, or other items to draw a visual link between that item and the shifting into a time of creativity. Give your eyes a place to direct their focus when concentrating.
- Engage through scent (candle, diffuser, flowers, etc.)
- Add or limit sound (music, nature, white-noise machine, or noise-canceling headphones).
- Enlist your sense of taste (tea, gum, a snack, etc.) or touch (a throw blanket, fidget, clay, sand, etc.) as other options as you create cues.

STEP 5
STOP WHAT'S STOPPING YOU!

The previous step serves to help you put your foot on the gas pedal and get moving. Yet some skills, when not held in check, operate more like the brake. They slow you down or bring you to a stop altogether. Next, let's consider some of the things that can pull you away from your plan and derail your focus. Everyone I know deals with distractions at some point. Some are external, coming from people, your surroundings, etc. But others come from within us. Procrastination and perfectionism may sneak in when you least expect it! Good self-management should include techniques that help you mitigate the things that stop you from putting your plan in motion.

Limit external distractions and interruptions.

Our brains are wired to react to distractions. It's a natural mechanism to pick up on threats and keep us safe. And while you likely don't have to deal with the physical dangers that our early ancestors did, the animal instinct is still there. It makes you aware of everything in your environment. You see how that can wreak havoc when you're trying to focus and get things accomplished! For that reason, it makes sense to mitigate distractions from happening in the first place. Put your biggest efforts into addressing the disruptions vs. fighting your natural response to listen and respond to those things that mentally interrupt you.

Is your environment a source of disruption? Consider all the factors at play—lighting, movement, temperature, noise, smells, seating comfort, workspace height, etc. People have different responses to their environments, and what one person considers an interference, another person can dismiss or ignore totally. Some people work well in coffee shops where a level of "white noise" and activity is easily tuned out.

Others find that atmosphere one of constant distractions as they watch people, hear conversations, and sense all the movement. If your physical space and location cause an interruption to your focus, consider what you can do to eliminate or lessen its impact.

People and even technology are additional sources of interruption. Some of those interruptions prove normal in a day, so stopping ALL of them probably isn't realistic. But you can take steps to decrease their occurrence and manage them when they happen. Here are a few ideas that cover each of those areas:

Physical Surroundings

- Move your workspace or the direction you sit/stand so that movement doesn't distract you.
- Wear noise-canceling headphones, play background music, or utilize a white noise machine to create a baseline of sound and block conversations or periodic noises.
- Adjust temperature if possible, or keep a fan/sweater on hand so you can adjust as needed.
- Look at the ergonomics of your furniture/tools to address comfort.
- Ensure sufficient task lighting is available.
- What is something in your environment that pulls your attention away from the task at hand? What can you do to change it?

People

- Shift your position so that it isn't easy to glance and catch someone's attention—others are much more likely to stop and chat once you make eye contact!

- Establish a visible sign to signal to limit distractions and interruptions. It can be a closed door, a posted sign, wearing headphones, or any other signal to let others know they should wait for a more opportune time to connect. Communicate well with those around you so that they understand the boundary you are requesting. NOTE: It's important to use that cue only during designated times. Giving others a message that you are not to be interrupted, but then leaving it up indefinitely, will make others unsure as to whether they really can sneak in "one quick question" or they may ignore your sign altogether.

- If seated, stand when someone interrupts you. It conveys that this isn't the time to stay and strike up a conversation. If you are the one walking by, ask them to walk with you to your destination (if you do have the time available while in transit). It also conveys that you are in the middle of another task, and the conversation should be brief.

- Practice using a phrase such as "I can't discuss this now but can be available ____." Or "Let's set up a time to talk so that I can give it my full attention." Develop a few phrases that feel natural and authentic to you. Don't allow your desire to be polite and helpful undermine your productivity. Equip yourself with ways to respond that tell them what you *can* do and *when* so that you honor your boundaries without brushing people aside or sounding unwilling to help.

- Schedule "office hours" when you openly communicate your availability to colleagues or staff. You can even earmark times for family and personal discussions. It might feel callous at first, but it sends a good message when you let people know you want to set aside time for them. It gives conversations and discussions a "home" in your schedule just as you'd assign an object a specific home in your home or office. It establishes clear parameters concerning your availability.

- Model the behavior you wish to receive yourself. Ultimately, we teach people how to interact with us. If you practice good boundaries around interruptions and distractions, people will begin to alter how they reach out. Provide people with a place and time to have needed conversations. Teach them to be proactive and thoughtful about the most effective way to meet and discuss things. Similarly, you can demonstrate the same approach as you interact with others. Limit the times you call out to a co-worker down the hall or stop by their office unannounced while working. Ask to set up times for discussions. Show respect for their time and model good parameters on your own.

Technology

- Pop-up notifications are great at keeping you up to date but are the bane of productivity. Unless you are highly skilled at fighting the urge to check messages and updates, it is a good idea to turn off notifications for all but the most necessary purposes. If you can't cut the cord fully on pop-up notifications, at least turn off the audible notifiers that can accompany them. Another option is setting up rules and sounds that only show up when specific people reach out so that calls from the boss or your child's school come through, but those from a colleague in the other branch office, or random solicitations or check-ins are held at bay.

- Incoming email is another common distraction. Like pop-up notifications, alerts for incoming emails can typically be adjusted or disabled. Some email platforms will allow you to only receive notices from specific senders, which is helpful to limit message notifications yet allows you to see critical messages from key people.

- Limit access to tools and apps that distract you most. If you are tempted by apps, websites, and systems, make them difficult to get to. Close out of those not in use, or try grouping icons and shortcuts by putting them on secondary vs. home screens. You may opt to remove access altogether for some platforms from some technology. Add extra layers to access them to lower the chances of being lured in.

- Invest time to learn frequently used tools. Unfamiliarity with software or applications used regularly can cause its own distractions by drawing your focus to figuring out *how* to do something instead of doing the work itself.

- Declutter your technology. Files and links can build up just like physical clutter. Pare down the items on your desktop and create clear paths to access the technology you use most. When there is less to wade through visually, you have fewer distractions to pull you away from the task at hand.

Perfectionism

One of the most common issues shared by clients and through my 6 Pillars Assessment is the admitted tendency to be a perfectionist. The intention to do something well is admirable and shows a focus on quality. It feels *right* to want to make things perfect. And at times, it's vital to invest your best energy toward creating the highest quality output possible. Where that positive intention turns into a hindrance is when you suffer the side effects of the hard work to make things *perfect.* **Perfectionism can cause a lot of collateral damage.**

Perfectionism impacts your efficiency by aiming for an area beyond excellence and striving for zero margin of error. It exponentially increases the time normally required to get the job done. Limitless hours can be spent on research, gathering information, fine-tuning, tweaking, and revising. It can impact other areas as well. An activity that should be delegated may not be when it's felt that losing control of the activity reduces its chances of being done to the highest standards. Procrastination can result if the task is delayed for a future time so it can get your sole attention when all options are weighed or to avoid what feels like a gargantuan task. The quality of the finished product may also suffer when too much time is spent gathering info, researching, or planning, and little time remains to complete the task well. Even time awareness is altered as absorption in the task at hand inflates the time spent and excludes other activities from getting the attention they deserve.

To address perfectionism, you don't need to eliminate all the times you aim for your highest quality work. Sometimes that's appropriate. What does address perfectionism is recognizing an activity's value and identifying an appropriate amount of time and energy to invest in it. As you look at a task, ask yourself:

- What is the impact of the work at hand?
- Who is the audience to receive it?
- Are the stakes high?
- What are the risks if it is done well vs. being perfect?

Consider the level of importance of the task. This level of importance isn't an invitation to do sloppy work but an opportunity to alleviate the stress of perfectionism when you acknowledge that not all activities carry the same weight regarding the need for a perfect result. Where perfectionism is identified, try these strategies to reduce or eliminate its frequency:

Identify the Perfectionism habit. What's in it for you? What drives that need to invest so much time to aim for flawless results? Perhaps initial efforts toward high standards have morphed into a perfectionism habit. Is there a sense that the bar is set so high that you have no room for anything less than perfect? Who set that bar? A habit links an action or thought with an outcome. Consider what you *get* when you feel you've done something perfectly. Is it a boost to your self-esteem, relief (or euphoria) that you've dodged a threat, or did the extra work of perfectionism allow you to push aside another, less appealing activity? Where do you see trends involving this tendency?

Clarify, before you begin, what it means to do this task well and thoroughly. Perfectionism can pull your thinking to the far end of the spectrum so that you believe it is of utmost importance that all things be flawless. Gather input to understand what an acceptable result can look like. Set a definitive finish line at an appropriate and achievable place.

Establish guidelines. Define for yourself some basic "rules of thumb" you can use to help you achieve excellent results without going well beyond the energy and time warranted. Examples can be determining how much time you'll spend on preparation and info gathering, setting a cap on how many options you need to research or evaluate, or recognizing that a first draft needn't be as thoroughly edited as a final version. Another helpful technique is defining what it looks like to have done "too much," and milestones can help as well. If you have one week to accomplish a task, consider where you should be in the process by the end of the day or by mid-week. You'll see more easily when you get off track and adjust before you are up against a deadline.

Practice imperfection. Yes, this can feel incredibly risky and uncomfortable to someone impacted by perfectionism! However, it is a direct route to experiencing what lies on the other side. Select a small task that is not tied to a high-value payoff. Is there a step that you could omit? Could you stop just shy of where you might have gone if the goal was "perfect"? That could mean you eliminate that one last review of a document or email before sending it to a colleague, or perhaps you simply leave your bed unmade or dishes in the sink so you can leave the house on time for an appointment. Afterward, focus not only on the feeling of discomfort for what was undone but also on the outcome.

- What/who was impacted?
- Were there negative consequences?
- Did you remember or even think about the missed final step or imperfection once you moved on to the next activity?
- Repeat this process periodically. The goal is not to BE imperfect but to ALLOW imperfection to exist while still acknowledging success.

   For some, perfectionism may stem from a condition such as obsessive-compulsive disorder (OCD) or another condition, which means additional care and attention should be given, typically within the guidance of a specialist trained in that condition. Mindfully consider how you can begin to practice this without causing self-harm or negative impact.

Manage Procrastination

The first step to managing procrastination is to **understand what it is and what it isn't**. It's a term usually given to any activity that doesn't happen when you initially planned. While procrastination may be the culprit, there are many other legitimate reasons that tasks get delayed.

New priorities or urgencies may have entered the scene, something needed to take the next step may not be ready, or problems could have occurred. Each of these can make it necessary to change the original plan. It could also be a conscious decision to take another direction with your use of time. When postponement comes from a place of choice or necessity, I don't refer to that as procrastination. It is the active work of re-prioritizing and decision-making throughout the day, as discussed earlier in this chapter. This clarification is an important distinction to make since the guilt of procrastination weighs heavily on many people.

Where true procrastination comes into play is when activities are paused, set aside, or ignored as a reactionary response, with the delay having a negative impact—missed deadlines or payments, insufficient time to do something or to do it well, missed opportunities, etc. Yet, despite these downsides, we all procrastinate sometimes. Over the years, clients have shared with me their reasons. Just a few of those are below. There is truth here, but they also mask something that is going on below the surface.

- I wait till the last minute because I work better under pressure!
- I just don't feel like it.
- This is going to take more time than I have right now.
- I need to get everything ready before I can begin.
- I shouldn't be the one having to do this in the first place!
- I'm not sure where to start.

So, what's *really* going on when you procrastinate? Getting down to the next layer of understanding gives insight. You see the core of the problem. Procrastination is simply your response to that problem. Address the root cause and you CAN tackle procrastination!

Is there something about the task itself causing your hesitation? The standard response many have is to internalize the reasons it is happening as a personal weakness or character flaw. Yet the obstacle may be the task itself. Is it complicated, problematic, or difficult? If you anticipate difficulty ahead or anticipate hurdles, it's easy to see why you'd shy away from a task. To make matters worse, when you dread a task, it feels bigger than it may truly be and usually results in over-estimating the amount of time the activity will require. That furthers the cycle when you delay the task until you have "enough time" to complete it. To find an example, look at your own experiences. Have you ever finally addressed something you've been putting off, only to realize it didn't take as long as you thought it would? You may have spent more time worrying about it than it took to actually get it done.

Is it a task or part of a project/series? A task is singular. It stands on its own, and when it is on your agenda for the day, you can move ahead. A project or series, however, represents something larger where multiple actions or steps must happen, sometimes in a specific order. When parts of the series are delayed, you can't do what you set out to do. To illustrate, I'll share an example of how this played out with a coaching client. We looked at a task that had been bypassed on multiple days. On the surface, it seemed straightforward—send an email regarding an upcoming event. The task itself was specific, would not require a lot of time, and was not difficult. However, as we talked about what stopped her from acting on it in the moment, she shared that it involved first locating an original email that held some pertinent information. She then needed to have a brief conversation with someone to clarify details. THEN she would have all she needed to do the task she initially planned. Her task list included only the last piece in the series but didn't acknowledge the first steps.

Is the delay/avoidance coming from within? Is there something going on internally that causes you to stall? These issues can be trickier to uncover and may not be something of which you're consciously aware. They deal with our reactions to people, experiences, self-doubt, level of interest or engagement in the activity, and sometimes our feeling overwhelmed. It explains why common steps to tackle procrastination may not work at times—they address the task but not our emotions about it, which is why procrastination is sometimes referred to as "mood management." Whether it's the task itself or your response to doing the task, try these techniques to thwart procrastination:

Regularly look back. I shared earlier the value of reviewing prior weeks for lessons we can learn and use going forward. It's a window into our actions and reactions. Don't only focus on what you are procrastinating on today. Look for trends concerning previous activities stalled. Each week, look back at the things left undone or those that set off negative emotions. Where have you seen repeated issues with procrastination? What was impacting your ability to launch an activity? Make this reflection a regular part of your weekly planning so you can address root problems and get those tasks done!

Determine how to Eat the Elephant! Desmond Tutu is credited with saying that the only way to eat an elephant is one bite at a time. That approach helps us tackle procrastination by breaking down larger projects or series into their individual components, steps, or tasks, as well as addressing the internal issues that cause us to delay or avoid them. Look at areas where you lack information/knowledge that would allow you to move forward. Get it out of your head and document it on paper or even a whiteboard. Once you can visualize it, look at the various pieces to assess any trouble spots or hurdles you might encounter. Any of these can lead to procrastination. The following table provides a few of the common struggles and ideas to address them:

The Struggle:	Try one of these:
Are you uncertain about HOW to do the task? Do you doubt your skills or knowledge?	Who has done this activity before? Can you get help from them?
	What questions come to mind? Who can help you get answers?
	Are there resource documents or reference materials available? Who may have that info? Look online.
	What are your options? What are the various ways you could begin? Write it out or talk through various scenarios to look for insight.
	Where could you get training to gain the knowledge you need?
	What is the cause of the uncertainty? Training, expectations, abilities, etc.?
Are you unsure where to begin?	Write down all the actions you need to take, questions you have, etc.
	Must some steps happen in order? What comes first? Which steps come later or require other steps to be completed first?
	Which actions are possible to take now?
	Where could you look for guidance on the best way to begin?
	Focus on the NEXT step to take vs. getting bogged down on ALL the steps that have to happen.

Is it hard to get motivated or engaged in this activity? Do you find the task boring, unpleasant, or uninteresting?	What part of the activity spurs this response? Is it only one part of the process causing the holdup? Is it possible to delegate or remove this activity? We sometimes forget to explore options for outsourcing activities we don't enjoy or aren't our strengths. Can you find a way to "gamify" the activity by finding a creative way to make it more engaging or fun? Look for something about the task to be curious about. What part of this task is new, exciting, or interesting? Find a reward or perk to give yourself when the step/task is complete!
Does it feel overwhelming?	Ask, "Why?" Keep asking, "Why?" You can get down to the root issue that's keeping you stuck. Don't look ahead at all the steps—identify the "next step" and work to address that one thing. Identify the smallest step you can take to get started. Often, once you begin, it is easier to continue. Talk it through. Find a colleague, friend, or family member with whom you can talk through the activity. You may be able to move beyond being overwhelmed when you verbally process with someone you trust.

Get individual steps scheduled in your weekly plan. The more specific you can be, the more manageable it feels, and the less likely you'll overestimate the effort or time it will take to get done. You can also set a time goal. For example, take 15 minutes to begin the first draft of that proposal or start the slides for your presentation. Notice that the goal isn't to finish—it's to **start**. When you limit the time, it feels more manageable than aiming to tackle the entire project. The goal is to provide yourself with a prompt that directs the exact activity needed so that it becomes as straightforward as possible. Try to make it as easy to simply DO the task as it is to reason yourself out of it.

STEP 6

OPTIMIZE YOUR WORK WITH OTHERS

Whether you work or live alongside others, be it family, colleagues, or even clients, chances are good that opportunities exist to be more productive through and with those relationships. Each intersection of your daily life with those around you is a place to explore options for leveraging your skills and even developing those of others.

Delegate

Some perceive delegation as a tool only to be used when you have staff or a direct report. In reality, it can be applied in a much broader sense. It can be applied in both your job and your personal life. As you consider whether to delegate an activity, what's your first reaction? Does it feel like a cop-out to simply offload your work onto someone else? Are there tasks you're resistant to pass on to others even when it's clear it should be done by another person? In truth, delegation is about aligning work and tasks with those best suited to do them. It leads to a larger reserve of focus and energy for those activities you find most valuable. It requires forethought, and there are steps to doing it effectively.

- **Get to the root of your hesitation.** Below are things I frequently hear clients say when first bringing up the idea of delegating some of their activities:
- **It's faster if I just do it myself!** The argument that holding onto a task is quicker than passing it on to someone else might be true in the short term but often proves false when you consider the long-term benefits, especially if it is a recurring activity. There might also be an emotional response at play when you dive into an activity so that you can "check it off the list," or it feels better to know it will get done the way you prefer.
- **I've been "burned" in the past.** If you've delegated a task in the past where the individual didn't follow through or provided incorrect or less-than-expected results, it makes sense that you wouldn't want to repeat it. Like touching a hot surface, the message that lingers is, "Don't do THAT again!" The fault with this logic is that bad past experiences needn't guarantee a negative future result when delegation is done well. Of course, delegating moves the activity to someone else and shifts control to the receiver. That remains a scary thing. But there are steps you can take to improve the delegation process and monitor progress to alleviate unpleasant surprises.
- **I enjoy the activity and want to keep it instead of giving it away.** This argument can be one of the hardest to get around. When you enjoy a task, it serves as a mood booster or a pleasant distraction from more arduous activities with less appeal. Sometimes it

provides a nice mix of activities to your day. There will always be a combination of fun and not-so-fun tasks on our plate. Where delegation comes into play is when necessary and relevant tasks aren't getting done, yet you're holding onto some that don't need to be done by you. A conscious decision should identify which tasks are worth keeping on your plate and where your overall productivity would be better served by relinquishing the task elsewhere.

- **Monitor delegation opportunities.** Before we consider *what* to delegate, let's think a bit about *who* might take on those responsibilities. I encourage you to think outside the "office" box. Delegation usually comes to mind in the context of work or the office. It's a logical line to draw since job titles define those to whom you can assign tasks and responsibilities, yet it doesn't need to stop there. Remember, delegation is the intentional activity of re-assigning oversight to a more appropriate person. That could mean enlisting a family member, a colleague, a committee member, or even an outside paid resource where appropriate. The challenge is to broaden your thinking. Don't consider yourself limited if you don't have employees or a designated backup. Who around you could benefit from learning a new activity, who is ready to take on new responsibilities, and who has a strength in an area you lack or would be willing to lend a hand? You may have more resources at your disposal than you initially considered.

As to timing, don't wait until your time and energy are maxed out before you put delegation into play. In fact, it's more beneficial to do this work before you get to that place so that there is time to give it forethought and mitigate that argument of having too little time to train someone else when you're already pushed to the limit. Periodically scan the horizon of your activities and consider if they belong with you. Here are a few questions you can ask yourself:

- Does it require my specialized knowledge, skillset, or experience?
- Is my contribution or management of the activity needed?
- Are there now others who could get involved that perhaps weren't available at an earlier time?
- Which activities have the least payoff or reap fewer results? Typically, a few key areas provide the biggest payoff in any role. If you were to spend most of your time on these, what activities would be left?
- Which tasks require skills that are *not* your strong suit? Is there someone that could do this more easily, quickly, or efficiently?
- Look at tasks you tend to procrastinate on. Ask why. Is it an option to reassign work that you don't enjoy?
- Could this activity help another person grow and develop? Is a maturing child ready to take on the next level of responsibility? Could a work project help develop and train a staff member? Can committee responsibilities be shifted to accommodate an individual's skills more effectively?

Delegate effectively through these steps. Delegation takes attention and management even after you've matched the task to its delegate. It's wonderful when we can easily transition an activity to someone else who immediately understands the full scope and can complete the request in the given timeframe. However, it doesn't always happen that way. A new activity with new expectations means there will be a learning curve, and clarification is often needed. Here are eight steps to help you manage the delegation process with effective results:

1. **Communicate the *task* as well as the *result* you expect.** It's easy to get wrapped up in stating the activity you want someone to do or outlining the steps to take. Sure, that's part of it, but it's also important to clearly state the end goal. Go beyond *how* to do the task and include details on the big picture. What should the finished product accomplish or need to look like? What is the purpose or outcome needed? Is the task part of a larger project? Who is impacted by the result?

2. **Adjust your thinking.** No two people do a task entirely the same way. Where is there leeway for the receiver to handle things differently? What steps of the process are important to follow exactly, and which can be adjusted? Always keep in mind that **what you are delegating is a result**. Clarify where people can develop their own process and have the flexibility to adapt to their own work style. They may interject areas where they see opportunities to improve or offer new perspectives. This step encourages you to enter the delegation process with an open mind.

3. **Determine what information, access, training, or resources the person will need to utilize.** Review these as you discuss the task to be delegated and identify where there are knowledge or resource gaps. Give direction on where to find the support, training, or tools that may be needed. Be proactive here so the responsibility does not rest solely on the delegate, as this can cause further delays and hesitancy to step forward and ask for help.

4. **Provide examples if available.** When someone can visualize and experience the result, it gives more understanding of expectations. If an example is unavailable, clarify what does and does not meet expectations. Pictures are helpful when the project needs to look a certain way, and checklists or procedures help when things are multi-step jobs.

5. **Consider "shadowing."** Shadowing is when the learner works alongside you or assists with the activity before taking it on fully. Let them observe in the beginning. Next, allow them to take on part or all of the activity themselves while you observe. This gradual integration works well with tasks that are already being done with some regularity. It helps train them fully and shows you if they are ready to take it on independently. It can also flag areas where further assistance is needed before they can take on full ownership of the task.

6. **Gather questions.** Together with the delegate, scan the project and ask questions such as:

    - What questions come to mind?
    - Where might there be hurdles or challenges in taking on the task?

- Where do you need me to provide support?
- How does taking on this task impact other work or responsibilities?"
- This opens a dialog to discuss areas of uncertainty in a way that is collaborative. It goes beyond asking, "Do you have any questions?"

7. **Agree on a timeframe for the work.** Is there a deadline? Are there milestones set to mark when parts of the work should be accomplished? Look outside the task itself to see if other things may impact the task being done in the timeframe needed. Especially when something is new, build in time to allow for hurdles or delays. Try to set a pace that allows quality focus and the necessary time to learn and understand the new activity.

8. **Set a check-in date or follow-up meeting.** Establish a time well in advance of any due date to check on progress, allow for more dialog and questions, and to monitor progress. This follow-up can be a simple email check-in, a reminder of the upcoming deadline, a request for regular updates, a meeting or call to discuss progress, etc. How much time to invest here is largely dependent on the size and importance of the task. As the delegate learns and becomes more independent, your involvement and oversight can be eased. It is after the task has fully transitioned that you can benefit from the real investment in effective delegation.

Improve your communications.

Unless you live and work in a solitary environment, communication absolutely plays a role in your efficiency. It goes beyond the words you say and the questions you ask. Much of a message is tied up in the *way* you communicate—your language, the content, timing, and whether it's in-person or via technology. Communication skills uphold your productivity when you:

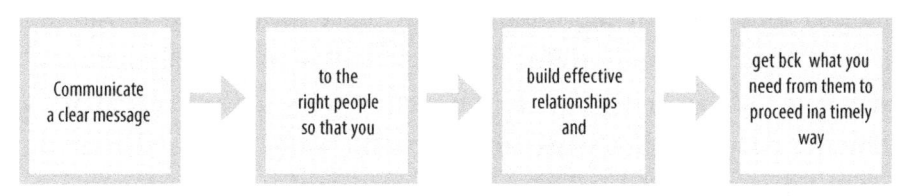

Communicate a clear message	→	to the right people so that you	→	build effective relationships and	→	get bck what you need from them to proceed ina timely way

While you can't control how others receive your messages and whether they respond appropriately, you *can* take steps to improve the chances that your messages land as intended and prompt any necessary responses. Honing your communications smooths the way for improved cooperation and increases the chances that what you need to accomplish through those communications will be achieved.

Here are a few places I see communication challenges crop up, along with considerations for making those interactions most effective:

Email. Managing email is one of the most time-consuming activities for many of us, so it is worthwhile (and appreciated by recipients) when those messages are concise, clear, and relevant. Know that the message may be skimmed or retrieved later when there is time to address questions. Formatting can go a long way to highlight specific points, dates or deadlines of notes, and questions you are asking.

Meetings. Make the most of meetings so that, like email, they are seen as practical and helpful. Honor start/end times, invite only those whose attendance is needed, know the meeting's purpose (is it to brainstorm ideas, provide information or updates, get status updates, etc.), and clarify next steps or future meetings either at the end of the meeting or with a follow-up recap.

Communication "Styles." We each have a unique communication style. Some prefer to cut to the chase; others consider interactions to be about building relationships. Within those styles, everything from body language, eye contact, volume, and the pace of speech matter. Communication becomes more fluid when we try to understand one another and meet in the middle when those styles vary. If you are a more direct communicator, but your colleague is relational, you may come off as being curt if you simply walk up and ask about a looming deadline. Likewise, someone who wants to spend time up front visiting or touching base before getting down to business may be viewed as wasting time or frivolous by those who prefer to get to the point. Being aware of your differences can help clear the way to open communications so that people don't "shut down" or even avoid discussions or collaboration. You don't have to overhaul your style, but taking steps toward the center can go a long way to making those relationships more effective and efficient.

Listening skills. Being a good communicator is a two-way street. If you are busy thinking about what you plan to say next, you can't be open to hearing or seeing the messages you get from others. Not only should you listen to the words, but also to what someone may *not* say. Body language is very telling. Could you improve your relationships by being a better listener?

LEVERAGE: HABITS & SELF-MANAGEMENT

KEY TAKEAWAYS

These habits and skills aid you in monitoring and controlling your actions and attention. It is about FOCUS.

Each of the following areas can impact your skills in this area. Where are you strong, and which may need improvement?

Internal Dialog

Habits—which support you, which are hindering you?

Working the Plan—are you referencing and relying on the roadmap you designed for your week?

Building and Maintaining Focus

Limiting external Distractions—your surroundings, people, technology Prioritizing & Decision-Making

Delegation

Manage Procrastination

Activation

Perfectionism

Improving your Communication

Which two topics above, if improved, would have the biggest impact on your productivity?

1.

2.

What specific steps will you take toward strengthening these?

PILLAR 5
ARRANGEMENT

WHEN YOU LOOK around your workspace, what do you see? Is it a neat freak's dream without a single sheet of paper in sight? A seemingly good thing—unless you can't easily find what you need on your computer. Or do you have piles of papers and folders stacked on all available surfaces? You know where to find what you need, but all the clutter overwhelms you.

Maybe you fall somewhere in between: your space looks neat and tidy, but you don't know how to easily find what you need because you haven't given much thought to where things should go. And so, you waste time churning through the clutter, searching for things.

Arrangement—how you set up your surroundings—may not be something that immediately comes to mind when you think of time management or productivity. But an environment that's not arranged optimally impacts our ability to get things done efficiently. You find yourself wasting time—time that could be spent being productive. This pillar does some heavy lifting. It provides support to hold up the roof. Having a strong Arrangement Pillar is crucial to our overall effectiveness.

Layout and order within a space drive its functionality. With this Pillar, we'll focus on setting up effective areas so you can **maximize**

your prime real estate and find what you need when you need it. It goes well beyond a space simply "looking tidy."

Arrangement is about organization—applying logic to the area in use. Understanding how an area will be used and by whom, what activities will happen there, equipment in use, storage needs, work style preferences of the primary user, ergonomics, safety, and even aesthetics are all factors to be considered. Planning how the space will be used goes beyond determining where things will go and considers how simply you can access those things you use most frequently.

For many, when we set out to arrange and organize, we think about those things we can touch, pick up, use, or see. But in recent years, there's another factor has been added to the mix: the explosion of information and records that now exist online and in digital form. For that reason, the arrangement of our data and information is also at play. Retrieval is key here as well. Can you find what you need? Additionally, there must be effective backup and maintenance to keep stored information safe and secure. Risk exists when technology is upgraded, platforms or applications cease to exist, subscriptions expire, backups fail, or inconsistent filing and storage are applied. Many of the strategies throughout this section apply to both physical and digital arrangements, but we will cover more on digital organization specifically later in this section.

THE BENEFITS OF A STRONG ARRANGEMENT PILLAR

You aren't alone if you've not thought about Arrangement—or organization—as a productivity factor. In fact, it's easier to recognize its value when considering the alternative. Disorganization has a huge impact on our time, so it stands to reason that organization is an important component for improved effectiveness. For that reason, Professional Organizers often work with clients on time management skills in conjunction with helping them organize their homes, offices, or digital records. If you've established well-organized spaces and the skills of Arrangement come naturally to you, you likely see and benefit from those strengths.

You Know This Pillar is Strong If...

You quickly access what you need.

Those with strong organizational skills are good at recognizing effective systems for an item's active use, storage, and maintenance. That translates to things having a "home" in the space—whether physical or digital—at any point in its use. Proficient organizers can trust the order they establish and quickly find what they need. When you are ready to launch into your day or start a project, you can quickly access what you need to get the job done.

You don't waste time with "do-overs."

Where organization is lacking, chaos tends to creep in. Restarting work on projects and tasks you've already begun—but can't find—is frustrating and wastes time. That can lead to lower-quality work due to time constraints, stress, guilt, and even low self-esteem. Strength here means there is less time spent in that place of chaos and duplicated effort.

You focus on things that matter.

Organized individuals tend to have a strong sense of what should and shouldn't be accessible in their prime real estate—the areas easiest to access. They will establish storage and a workflow to accommodate those needs. When items are stored within those systems, there is less left to pile up as extra "clutter." Effective organization considers what is visible in the space, ensuring it channels attention and focus on what keeps you on track.

You save money.

For those who have strong organizational skills and keep things maintained, items and information have a home. Finding things when you need them is easy. You save money by eliminating unnecessary purchases and the wasted time expenditure caused by searching for, re-creating, and managing things.

You maximize your space.

When things are arranged and stored efficiently, you need less space. To illustrate, picture an overflowing laundry basket. If everything is simply tossed inside, it's hard to distinguish much beyond the top layer. However, once folded, the size of the stack is smaller, and it's much easier to see what it holds. So, how does this translate to your time? The efficiency gained when you store items in an organized manner means less space is needed to maintain order, AND more will be able to fit within the prime real estate available. A capable organizer can "do more with less" and keep things accessible and usable, all within a minimum footprint of space.

How Does Your Arrangement Pillar Hold Up?

A disorganized space isn't just a symptom of this Pillar being weak; it's a by-product as well. The opposite can also be true: A tidy space isn't necessarily an indication that this Pillar is strong. Signs that this Pillar may need reinforcement can include the following:

- Lost documents/information
- Distracting clutter
- Piles of Items with nowhere for them to go
- A workflow that isn't working
- Needed items are not kept where you use them

This Pillar is notorious for its visible symptoms. Disorder in our environment can vary from your typical day-to-day clutter as you live

Arrangement

and work in your space to more extreme situations where accumulation and lack of order reign. Simply put: Things get messy! And we're not just talking physical stuff. These days so much of our lives reside in the digital realm. Like a paper document being lost within stacks, digital documents can be inadvertently saved to incorrect folders, assigned names that hinder their search-ability, or sit lost within email chains. If you've heard yourself frequently saying, "I know it's here somewhere," when trying to locate documents or information, that's a sure sign that your Arrangement and organization need a tune-up!

Getting distracted by messiness is another common issue. People vary greatly in how much they can tolerate within their line of sight without it interfering with their ability to focus. Having items pile up and accumulate turns even useful and necessary items into "clutter" when they are not needed for the task at hand. Working amidst this clutter means there are more visible cues to process every time you see them. A stack of paper becomes not just a stack of paper but a reminder of a project that awaits your attention, a volume of reading or work you're not doing, or the possibility that something important has been buried or overlooked. Have you avoided inviting others into your space? Have you experienced guilt when you see tidying left undone or felt frustration at decisions waiting to be made? It's easy to see why even a quick glance around you can trigger distracting thoughts when in a disorganized space.

When I work with clients to organize an area, we begin by searching for clues together while studying the space. How did things end up where they are? There's no judgment here—we're fact-finding. Are items awaiting action? Do things need to be put away or forwarded to someone else? Are you frequently uncertain about where something should go next? If accessible storage and "containerization"—a fancy word Professional Organizers use to identify where things live and what holds them—are lacking, things can pile up or get set aside as new work commences. The problem goes beyond occasional tidying-up sessions to put things back in order. We all need to do that periodically. A bigger question to ask is, do you have a system in place with which you can catch up? Reminder—even organizational systems that work today need frequent (or at least occasional) updating. What worked five years ago may not work at all as your job/duties/projects evolve.

A well-arranged space is more than aesthetics or how it *looks*. I've seen a minimalist space where the owner couldn't locate anything, and I've seen the other extreme—a packed office where the user knew exactly where to find everything. Good arrangement must consider function. The layout of any area should work well for the activities that occur there. Disorganization disrupts that effectiveness.

Historically, some of the earliest studies on productivity were tied directly to organization. In agriculture, studies looked at how best to organize equipment usage, hire the right kind of workers at the right time, and ensure transportation was ready to pick up and deliver the crops at the optimal time. Organization of all these components is still practical and necessary.

In the industrial and manufacturing sectors, they found that output could be maximized by limiting waste of materials and movement by ensuring all needed items were close at hand and utilized to their full potential. Today we see examples with automotive plants, the package delivery industry (think FedEx or UPS), and Amazon, to name a few. How they organize their floorplans, assembly lines, and delivery hubs is what has catapulted the growth of these businesses. It is imperative that they have their Arrangement down pat if they want to maintain their competitive edge.

Even if your current role doesn't measure productivity by looking at the number of widgets produced or minimizing the movement required to get your work done, these examples still highlight the value that Arrangement can have on our use of time. Let's look now at ways you can strengthen and reinforce this Pillar.

ARRANGEMENT IN ACTION
TIPS & TECHNIQUES

Sometimes organizing gets a bad rap. People feel guilty as if they are taking the time that should be spent doing something else *productive*. They might not see the relevance of how it impacts their use of time. Others aren't sure where to begin or just want to avoid their "mess." But, if you give it the attention it deserves, the payoff can be huge. In all my Professional Organizing career, I have never had anyone at the completion of a project say that they regret investing the time to organize. In fact, most tell me they LOVE IT or at least love the result! The process is cathartic, and being able to see the results is gratifying. Just as lists are useful to "clear the clutter" in our minds, organizing can be great—and practical—therapy to improve your efficiency. When you break the ice and start to see order and purpose emerge, you recognize the tangible benefits.

Find a partner to help with the process. It can speed up the work and provide a viewpoint separate from your own to help you think through the project. You may have friends or family that can lend a helping hand. Just be sure to make that partner someone who will provide support and help you achieve *your* vision and needs. Professional Organizers are a great resource. We specialize in working with individuals to arrange your space and set up systems. Whether you opt to go it alone or enlist the help of a friend or professional, the tips and techniques covered here can get you started to reclaim a work area that provides true support for all you need to do.

STEP 1

IDENTIFY AND ADDRESS "CLUTTER"

As a Certified Professional Organizer®, I've had many discussions with clients about clutter. If there's one thing I've learned, it's that this simple word—clutter—has a wide variety of definitions and understandings. When clients talk about their clutter, they sometimes share frustration, guilt, or even shame over being unable to tackle it themselves or not addressing it earlier. They perceive the clutter as unnecessary, useless, or even junk. Standard dictionary definitions of clutter include words and phrases such as "untidy," "scattered," "disorderly," "messy," "too many things," etc. It usually ties the combination of a large amount of "stuff" that is piled up or strewn about chaotically. Notice it does *not* imply or assume that all clutter is junk. It means that even the most useful items, when allowed to accumulate without order, can become clutter. I feel that is an important distinction because it hits at the root of why addressing clutter can be a surprising challenge. It's bigger than clearing away unnecessary items. So, let's break down the job of identifying—and addressing—that clutter!

SEE the space.

In those rooms and workspaces where we spend time every day, you can become blind to your surroundings. Items that have long been on your counter or desktop fade into the background, and you don't see them anymore. You only recognize that there isn't much room to get anything done and that the space can feel cramped, stressful, and demotivating. Sound familiar? None of these are conducive to a productive mindset. A good place to start as you get organized is to take a step back and really SEE your space. The work to organize begins with awareness. Try one of these methods for a new perspective:

Take pictures. Photograph your desk, workspace, office, or area from a few angles. Then, move to another room and take a close look at the photos. What stands out? Any surprises? The way you sit, stand, and work in a space becomes routine. You may overlook things as they become part of your everyday background. This technique provides a new view and different perspective. There is something about viewing a picture vs. standing in the space that can open you up to see things in a new way.

Focus on one area at a time. Break down the job into smaller segments. You can focus on one small aspect at a time and still see incremental progress. Each day, pick a drawer, area, shelf, or stack. Do a quick assessment. The goal is to acknowledge what it holds. How much space can you free up by removing things that don't belong? Look for the opportunities that exist if that area is reclaimed from clutter.

Clear the area. Decisions on letting go, as you declutter and organize, always seem harder than decisions on what to keep. This technique takes a broad sweep to remove everything from the space and allows you to focus on the positive side of selecting what will earn its way back in. **What truly belongs in this newly opened space? What do you need around you as you work to keep you most productive?** Note that this work can take a lot of space to accomplish and might feel overwhelming since it means clearing most items from the area while you work. You can decide if that will include large items such as furniture or only the smaller contents. If you're ready to commit to the organizing project that will follow, clearing the area allows you to start with a blank slate. If space is limited and emptying everything all at once is unrealistic, you can still use this approach but work in one "zone," such as a single closet, desk area, toy storage, cabinet, etc., at a time.

Edit what doesn't belong.

Don't use time, energy, and resources to organize things that ultimately don't belong in the space, are no longer needed, or have a home elsewhere. To begin, make room to set these items aside for now and gather a few tools to aid the editing process. Have bags or bins ready to hold trash, shredding, and recycling. Gather containers for items you will be moving or donating and have paper or post-its on hand to label the action needed. Now, to make some decisions regarding what doesn't belong—as you view things with a critical eye, determine if you can say:

I can toss this! If it's trash, outdated, broken, antiquated, one of multiple, unnecessary, accessible in digital files or online, or you didn't even remember you had it until you started looking through things, then it can likely be removed permanently. Warning: purging can become addictive! While I'm an advocate of "less is more," don't get carried away to the point that you take chances and toss items that will likely be needed later or for which there is no backup. It can be a good idea to set some parameters before you begin. Are there guidelines about document retention? Does someone else deserve input on what is kept? Can you decide to keep it only until a replacement is received or a new version is created?

I need this—but I don't know where to put it. Set it aside so that you can build in an appropriate spot for it when you design your overall workspace. We will come back to these items later.

This has a home—I just need to put it there. Things get pulled out when in use but sometimes don't get put away when finished. Items are put down and then forgotten. It happens. Life is busy. What's important to distinguish is what's behind it:

Does your space need a tune-up? It's ideal when your system and storage make it as easy to put things away as it is to leave them out. However, we all fall short of this goal sometimes. Build in time for regular upkeep or organizing sessions to get caught up and put things back where they belong. Needing a tune-up for a system that is working overall doesn't signal an issue with the system itself, just the need to allocate time occasionally to maintenance.

Is there something about the current system that makes getting items back where they belong problematic? Keep asking yourself *why*. Get to the root of what stops you. Is space limited? Maybe there isn't sufficient room for the volume of storage you have. Is it the logistics of getting the item back where it belongs? Is it needed frequently, but its home isn't within easy reach? Is visibility an issue? As you move into the work of thinking about and designing an effective workspace, strive to address those problems that can be remedied and understand what it will take to work around those that can't.

Is it time to purge? Even if you designate homes for items, that doesn't ensure unlimited space. Periodically, review your storage space to determine if it's time to cull through what it holds. Documents may only be needed for a period before they are irrelevant and unnecessary. Memorabilia such as vacation brochures or children's artwork may have been kept in abundance originally but can be filtered down to the favorites over time. Purging is a regular part of the organizing process. Evaluate if it's time to free up room for the new by removing some of the old.

It's all good. I just need to take this where it belongs. Maybe there isn't really a problem—there is somewhere for it to go, and there is room when it gets there. You just need to catch up on some putting away. Great! Enough said.

Avoid the "Now, what do I DO with it?" dilemma.

At this point, it's easy to fall into the trap of interrupting your progress to decide where all the items you've removed will ultimately go.

Remove quickly those that are trash, shredding, or recycling since their fate has already been made. For other items, such as those items that you'll move elsewhere, need to be put away, will be donated, or about which you are still unsure, further decisions are needed, and it is here that sometimes people become stuck.

If you halt the organizing process now to take items elsewhere, it breaks momentum and distracts you from the task at hand. Unless you are at a natural place to finish up for the day or space is too limited to work further until items are removed, I suggest you simply set these items aside. For now, select a few broad categories such as "put away," "return," "figure out later," or "donate." If the label gives you an adequate prompt, use whatever works for you. We've all gotten up to put something away in another room only to be distracted and lose sight of what we had been doing. Stop self-sabotage—stay on-task and save the "putting away" until you've reached a good stopping point.

You might experience another sticking point as you decide what to do with those items you intend to give away or donate. Again, don't let that stop the process now. Either at the onset of your organizing project or at its completion, consider any organizations, groups, or individuals who may benefit from receiving what you no longer need. Once you know who will receive your donations, it decreases the chance that bags and bins will linger in your space any longer than necessary. But don't linger too long on these decisions. It's great when you can easily match your items with the perfect recipient, but the key is not letting it derail you or your work to arrange a productive space. Lastly, schedule a time to get them there or load them in your car if possible. Better yet, arrange for a pickup service!

Not sure where to start looking for options? Many resources are available online if you search for donation sites in your area. Some will even offer to pick it up! Of course, this can't begin to capture all the options out there. Places such as libraries, schools & preschools,

Arrangement

nursing homes, consignment stores, or charities may accept donations for their use or resale/auction during fundraisers. Even social media sites can offer a place to share with your neighborhood or other groups when you may have things you are willing to pass along that others might find useful. If you don't have this all figured out at the start of your project, plan a time to decide afterward where these items will ultimately end up. That research may also prove helpful for future donations

STEP 2

SORT AND CATEGORIZE

Now that you've set aside or removed the items that don't belong, look at what's left—sometimes, what remains feels chaotic. That's why we identify categories as a logical next step. Sorting, at its most basic definition, is to put related items together. It's not about what to do with items or even how to organize them—yet. It's a fact-finding mission and there are many ways to go about it. If you already have a clear picture of the categories your belongings or information represent, this may not be a necessary step, or it's one you can easily tackle. Great! But for those who feel anxious, overwhelmed, or unsure about how to categorize or subdivide items, there are steps below for you to follow that will walk you through the process. The goal isn't perfection—it's to get your items segmented into distinct areas that make sense to YOU.

Make room for the sorting fall-out!

You're going to physically move items around and place them in various areas and stacks as you work to gather like items together. Clear some space for a work area where you can spread out. If room is limited, you may opt to use boxes or bins you can stack. This fall-out is the point where I let clients know that it will likely look worse before it looks better. Yet it's through the chaos that you will begin to find order.

Have paper or post-it notes handy for labeling.

Don't focus yet on what your labels need to say. Categories will come into focus later as you begin to group items and name them. If you have a lot to sort through or plan to tackle this in multiple sessions, things can lose clarity, so labeling zones and stacks helps. Have simple tools ready to easily create those temporary labels.

Pick a starting point.

I find it most effective to methodically work through the sorting process vs. randomly picking up items throughout the space and dealing with them haphazardly. Whether you pick a spot or zone to begin, work your way around the room or gather items together and start at the top of the stack. It's easier to see progress when you're intentional about tackling the project.

Start asking questions.

At this point, some people start to falter, thinking they should already know what to do with the item when they pick it up. Instead, **simply identify what the item represents.** The pressure is off to have answers at this point. In fact, I think this is where the magic happens, and this is some of my favorite work with organizing clients. As you look at each item, ask the following:

- **What is this item's purpose?** Is it here to remind you to do something? Is it a resource document you'll need in the future? Is it a tool or reference material you utilize frequently? Do you even need it anymore?
- **Does this item relate to a specific task or role you have?** Is it related to a particular category of work or

oversight? Some examples may be marketing-related items, a volunteer role, administrative tasks, notes or documents regarding an upcoming project, staff development, supplies for a specific activity, etc.

- **Is it related to a specific individual?** Perhaps you tend to group together all items related to your manager, child's school/teacher, or client.

- **Is there a random label or category that makes sense to you?** Some clients like to use a catchy term or phrase when they consider what a group of items represents to them. A file titled "Keep the CPA happy" may contain financial paperwork and receipts, or a bin labeled "Road Trip!" may hold travel accessories only used occasionally. There is no wrong way to group your items if it prompts appropriate recognition by the user of what it holds and what needs to happen with it.

Review the categories you created.

Is anything missing? Is this a good representation of the information, tools, documents, and resources you'd typically include in your area? What about volume? It's important at this stage to ask if there is a lot less or more in your space now than you'd typically have. Is there anything that deserves to be added and would be helpful to have closer at hand?

The next step in the process will be to put thought and planning into how you can best arrange your space. Seeing the categories you created and understanding the volume of space and storage those items require will be helpful as you arrange your space for maximum functionality.

STEP 3

PLAN YOUR SPACE WITH PURPOSE

I have found that even the smallest, most improbable work and storage spaces can be highly effective. Likewise, large spaces afford more layout and storage options, yet they can be under-utilized and impractical if not designed with purpose. Arranging a space with productivity in mind means you give consideration first to functionality and accessibility. As you move into the job of establishing areas for all the items you just finished sorting, let's hit on a few things to consider at the onset of any design:

Create an atmosphere conducive to work.

What environments do you find uplifting, energizing, and productive? What helps make a space more effective for you? Consider what has impacted you in the past—which components in your surroundings aid you in getting more done, and which have hindered your ability to focus and achieve? Are noise or visual distractions problematic? Do you have enough light? What is the aesthetic you want to employ—sleek lines, warm and inviting, etc.? The Chapter on Goals under "Setting the Stage" provides a lot of information and ideas for exploring what works best for you. Atmosphere can certainly have an impact, so it makes sense to consider it as you design and organize your space.

Use ergonomics for comfort & accessibility.

This is especially important for areas where you will spend large amounts of time. Not only does it address comfort, but also the long-term physical effects. Work to design a space that considers the ease of using the space both in the short and long term. Be kind to your body and consider traffic patterns, obstructions, workspace height, lighting, and body positioning when working or retrieving items. Even minor adjustments can boost your effectiveness by mitigating physical problems and making your space more comfortable and easier to work in.

What's your optimal layout?

Consider the overall layout of the space—whether a desktop workspace or the entire room or office. At a high level, this means the physical room/area, furniture, and fixtures. You can also drill this down to consider where items are housed on a desktop, counter, or within drawers. What components are fixed, and which could be changed? Think of the possibilities your space holds. You may opt to keep everything "as is" or only make small adjustments. Or you may opt for an overhaul to boost your use of space.

Maximize your prime real estate.

If you've ever purchased tickets to a concert or event, you know that ticket prices are higher for good seats. The same goes for real estate. Areas with the best views and proximity to all the action are premium and often get snapped up first. When you stand or sit in your main work area, consider yourself and your work as the main attraction. Which areas around you are worth a premium price tag? Where is your prime real estate? Typically, it's the range of space within arm's reach and most accessible. Avoid the pitfall of prime real estate being used as a convenient dumping ground or storage space simply because it is close at hand. I've seen plenty of offices that only have one main drawer or cabinet, yet it's used to house a handbag, snacks, or a former employee's files. This prime real estate is your best and most accessible space; align your most-used tools so that they reside here.

Consider how work "flows" through the space.

Think about how work takes place in your office or work area. It may help to visualize a specific type of document or item and track its path as it comes in and gets used. Where and how do items enter?

Where do they go when you're done with them? Is there an entry point (inbox)? Where do things tend to pile up? Is there space that is over or under-utilized? What is problematic about the space? What are its best features? All the factors you've experienced will help you make good choices and design a workflow that "makes the work flow."

Manage the paper.

While much of our file storage, communication, and work happen digitally, paper is still a factor when organizing your space, and for many people, it's their fiercest enemy! For some clients, this paper is focused on household records and bills, recipes, or children's schoolwork and artwork. For others, this is about personal notes and records, task lists, coursework, continuing education records, or company files. When it comes to productivity, I look beyond the paper's purpose and focus instead on *how you use it*. Is it something to be kept long-term? Is there a way to store it digitally, or is the best solution to find a home for the paper files? What about "working documents"? Are you someone who likes to physically hold paper when you read documents or make notes? I've known very few people who are paper-free. As you work to improve your organization, now is a time to think about the role paper plays for you, where a shift to digital storage could make sense, and when to accept the use of paper documents and tools when they prove effective for your work style.

The previous steps have led up to this point—to raise awareness and, hopefully, help you envision a layout that proves effective and efficient. People choose different ways to begin their design. Some choose a pencil and paper method by drawing out options on a floor plan or workspace layout. Engaging someone else to talk through different alternatives or design a layout is often helpful as well. Others like to roll up their sleeves and physically begin moving things around to try out different options. Professional Organizers excel at this type of work and can be strong allies throughout all phases for activities such as:

- purging and sorting
- helping you think through the categories, tools, and resources you use
- allocating your prime real estate appropriately
- maximizing your use of space
- setting up a workflow that is functional

An organized space allows simplified access and storage. Plus, it limits the clutter that can cause distractions and waste.

STEP 4
DESIGNATE A SPACE FOR EVERYTHING

Earlier steps to de-clutter, sort, and evaluate your current systems should provide a good sense of the items to remain in the area. We'll move forward with the assumption that, at this point, the work has been done to cull down anything that is not needed, and all that remains is pertinent. The next step is to decide on the most appropriate form and location for storage. What space do you have available? How much room is in your primary workspace? Is there availability for any long-term storage elsewhere? Do you have adequate containers? What types of space are available—hanging file storage, open drawers, shelves, credenzas or cabinets, bookcases, boxes, bins, or perhaps off-site storage? Even your desktop space can provide some storage—you just need to be judicial when deciding what goes where.

Assign "homes" for storage.

As you look at all items to be housed in your space, think about the types of work or activity they represent.

- Where and how can you keep action items (things you're currently working on) vs. items you can stow away till they are needed later?
- Which items make sense to group together?
- Do filing systems already exist online or in email that can be replicated for your physical items and documents? Are other things already grouped by client, project type, product, or even people, such as by supervisor or sales rep?
- Can you store things in zones to place related items together? Maybe one drawer is designated for HR files or financials, while another is for projects. Bookcases can be given zones so that it's easier to locate items based on their type or content. Desktop sorters and file trays may be used for "active" items by topic. The result is that you can look around your space and clearly identify what types of things belong in what types of areas. Make sure everything is represented and that you've reserved that prime real estate for the most-used items.

Items should be easily accessible.

How easily you can retrieve, view, use, and return things to their home is important to the functionality of the space. If location makes it a nuisance to get to something, or it's difficult or cumbersome to retrieve it, you're less likely to maintain it there. I've seen many piles and stacks attributed to the inconvenience of hole-punching items that should go in a binder, getting a storage bin down from a high shelf, or the need to fight with a desk drawer that's hard to open. Consider the ease with which you can get to items—especially those you use often. Also, the more frequent or current its use, the closer to your primary workspace it should be. Lesser used items can be moved further away and may warrant storage that is a bit less accessible to reserve premium space for those items that are more vital and timely.

Use Labels to aid retrieval and return.

There is a reason that labels are a "go-to" for Professional Organizers. Labels give visual cues as to where items can be found and where to put them away. They provide reminders to keep the arrangement in place so there is less chance you'll forget an item's home. The more people who access an area, the greater the benefit of effective labeling since everyone can be unified in understanding and maintaining the storage system. Even if it's yours alone, labels pay off in keeping an area organized. Based on your storage needs, determine if you can keep labels simple (i.e., label zones or areas) or if you wish to be specific (i.e., label shelves in cabinets, specific file folders, etc.) Is there much fluidity in the space where labels may have to be adjusted frequently? What about temperature? Items stored in a garage or non-temperature-controlled area may need a different adhesive so that labels don't fall off. Labeling can consist of simply writing on an item, adhesive printed labels, laminated pages, or sheet protectors to hold signage, flags, etc. When you start an organizing project, you may begin with more "temporary" labels such as heavy-duty post-it notes or even painter's tape. As you finalize your storage, move to more permanent labels that fit the space and visibility needs of the area.

Use quality tools.

I strongly suggest you invest in quality storage tools that aren't meant to be temporary. That doesn't mean they have to be fancy or expensive. It does mean that they are functional and will hold up under use. Here are a few considerations for storage tools I've seen used in both residential and office spaces:

Bins and Boxes: Containers not only serve the purpose of grouping items so they can be stored together, but they also streamline the visual space. Consideration should be given to where the container will be stored. Keep size relative to the amount of lifting needed to access it and the weight of its contents. Can it be easily labeled if needed? Are handles and lids sturdy and easy to grip? Would you benefit from having a clear container to better see the contents? Will the container remain visible, and if so, what aesthetics are important? Do the contents warrant special storage considerations, such as memorabilia and photos? Will the bins and boxes need to be sturdy enough to be stacked?

File storage: Make sure that file drawers have secure hardware inside so that rails to hold hanging folders are sturdy and won't come loose. Test the drawer by hanging both a hanging file AND an interior file folder within it. Is there plenty of clearance to close the drawer if full of files? Does the drawer slide easily, or does it get stuck or off track? Some credenza files allow you to store files either facing front (allowing two rows) or laterally. Make sure it will hold enough files to warrant the floor space that these pieces of furniture require. Also, make sure that file cabinets have the safety feature of allowing only one drawer to open at a time OR are secured to the wall to avoid tipping. Other storage options include file bins, boxes, accordion folders, and even rolling file holders. Think about the number of paper files you have, if mobility is needed, and if it feels sturdy enough to hold the weight when filled.

File Folders: While these seem to be one of the most basic supplies, there is quite an array available. Simple manila folders are a staple but consider bumping up your organizing game by utilizing color coding; larger, more visible tabs; choosing a specific tab location (left, center, right) to make files easier to see. Some file folders also have a non-slip coating making them easier to pull out of the drawer. What features could you benefit from having?

Desktop/Countertop containers and trays: These are often the most frequently accessed storage tools, so they should be sturdy and durable. Stacking trays need to be secure with little chance of slipping; they should feel capable of holding the weight when filled with items. Allow room so that if more is added, it can accommodate your needs. Don't fall prey to choosing your storage only because you like the way it looks. Make sure it addresses your storage needs first and aesthetics second. No matter how nice the design, it's just clutter if you can't use it.

Printed Labels: Label makers are a great tool as they are adhesive, provide different size fonts to improve visibility, and are coated so that they are easy to wipe off. Handheld options are good for basic homes and offices. If you anticipate a large amount of labeling will be done or if you want to create specialized sizes, look for options that allow different label tape sizes and have software to enable printing more custom labels via printer. Tip: Consider the cost of replacement label tape when selecting a label maker. The units themselves are often inexpensive, but the tape can get pricey. Beyond using a standard label maker, many types, shapes, and kinds of labels are available online. Office supply stores usually offer alternatives, but you may wish to do a broader search online for your specific needs.

Adhesive Labels: Labels can take many forms beyond label makers. Options can be found for nearly any size, color, or use. For labels that may change over time, some come with a plastic pouch into which labels can be inserted so they can easily be updated as contents change. Consider visibility, and utilize a font size that will allow it to be easily seen. The further up/down/away the label, the bolder the writing should be.

Tools of the Trade: Whether you are organizing your office, kitchen, garage, or virtually any other type of space, evaluate the key items in regular use. Invest in tools that will last and that simplify the job. Sometimes that means spending more upfront, but if it alleviates buying replacements or gets the job done quicker, it's easy to see how this can impact your time and space. What are the tools you grab regularly? Do they work well? Do you have to struggle with them? Is it time to replace substandard items with better options?

STEP 5

MAINTAIN IT ALL

Once the job to organize and arrange is completed, your tendency may be to back out of the room and never touch anything again lest you "mess it all up!" I've seen clients accumulate new piles of paper in the dining room because they didn't wish to clutter their newly tidy home office. Supplies sat on a counter because of uncertainty about how to make room for new projects. But what good is a well-arranged space if you're not going to use it? Things won't always look perfect. That's not how life works. How can you begin day-to-day use of a space without sacrificing order? What is the magic ingredient to make your arrangement stick? Maintenance!

Setting up simple yet effective systems and storage goes a long way toward maintaining your space day-to-day. But even simple systems get messy. That is why this final step is so vital. It's a good and necessary thing to do periodic "tune-ups." The good news is that once you've established homes for items and there's a logical layout to where things are kept, ongoing maintenance—whether done daily or only periodically—is a straightforward process. You may also see areas that need a bit of tweaking to be most effective or accommodate new needs. The following are some ways you can maintain your space and keep things from piling up.

Periodically purge items.

We don't need to keep everything forever. Some things get replaced when they are worn out, outgrown, or no longer used. Still, others have a "shelf-life." That may be literal, such as with food and medications, but think about things such as schoolwork, fire extinguishers, batteries, or even files containing reports, bills, or household maintenance records. For items like these, include the date or year so it's easy to recognize when it can be tossed. Labels can highlight items that need to be replaced periodically. Maintenance is easier when we simplify how to recognize those things that can be purged over time. How can you easily flag it so that a quick glance lets you know it's time for it to go?

Set limits on the space allowed or how much is needed.

Setting a maximum amount of space a certain item or category can occupy helps you maintain your systems. For instance, if magazines accumulate, select a basket or other container to hold them. Once full, something must be purged before a new item can enter. This limiting can also work with clothes (new item in, old item out), documents such as insurance policies (replace the old with the current policy so that you never have more than what is active), or even children's artwork (choose a box to hold that year's work then stick to the space allotment when deciding what to collect).

Question your need for multiples.

It's true that it can come in handy to have backups of items you use regularly. What hinders organization is when you maintain multiples beyond what is necessary. How many pens/pencils, tablecloths, sheet sets and towels, jackets, pans, coffee mugs, or pairs of black dress shoes seem reasonable for your needs? How many versions of that report need to be kept in hard copy? Everything we bring into our space requires some of our time and attention. Your productivity can be impacted when you must maintain more than is used regularly. Yes, it's hard to let go of things, especially when they are still serviceable. But ask yourself if your organization and ease of function are worth sacrificing in order to maintain duplicates and overabundance.

Ask, "Is it available elsewhere?"

Some items that have traditionally been held physically can be replaced with a digital record. Items such as appliance manuals and recipes can be easily found online, and most movies and music are available via streaming services. Are your paper documents copies of something already stored digitally? For those things that you would be more likely to access online, decide if the physical item is necessary to keep. This doesn't mean you need to sacrifice those things that prove useful to have in a tangible form, but it does encourage you to think differently. It's simply easier to maintain a space that holds less.

Ask, "What do I need to make room for?"

Maintenance isn't only about culling down. Life evolves, and that may mean making room for new things you're using now. Look around you. What items are in play today that weren't when you last organized your space? Do they deserve to have a home, or are they only there temporarily? Do you need to allocate more room to something that no longer fits its assigned space? Use a critical eye and make objects earn their way in. If they deserve to be there, take time to build them into your organizational plan.

Online & Digital Organization

Let's think now about belongings beyond your physical environment. As mentioned earlier in the section, the enormity of information and data available online and in digital form is huge. Just as the disorganization of your physical space can hinder productivity, the

Arrangement

same applies to virtual records, yet this often gets overlooked as it doesn't provide as many visual reminders when disorganized. Can you find electronic files and information when needed? Where does your data reside? What about photos? Is there a consistent location you keep your online files, or are things spread between different platforms?

Unlike physical things, you don't have tangible items, space limitations, or boundaries with digital records. You can't necessarily *see* all that you have. Unlike a large volume of hardcopy records, one digital file folder can contain endless interior folders and subfolders. Electronic records make it easy to send and update information, yet they can easily be misfiled or mislabeled and become hard to locate. The method to organize digital records is not vastly different from physical organizing—remove extraneous records, set up recognizable and relevant categories, and identify the best form/location for storage. What you'll need to accomplish first is to **identify all the places where your electronic information is currently located.**

Digital records have a multitude of places where they can be stored. Many people also end up keeping multiple copies of the same information. Here are some common locations:

- Computers/Tablets - (remember to consider older technology no longer in use but that may hold records on its hard drive)
- Cloud-based document storage (i.e., Box, Evernote, Google Docs, etc.)
- Email
- Backup drives (i.e., external hard drives, cloud-based backup, thumb drives, CDs)

- Workplace computers/servers
- Phones
- Applications and Software

Within all these various tools, **consider the *types* of information you regularly create, store, and utilize**. These are just a few examples:

- Digital Documents
- Downloads
- Pictures
- Website/Links/Favorites
- Backups
- Bookmarked articles, recipes, ideas, etc.
- Notes

Once you've identified **what** you have and **where** it is located, determine if records can be consolidated to streamline the location and maintenance of your digital records. It may still make sense to use multiple places for different types of info but put some thought behind their location and select those locations with intention. Like physical organization, helpful steps are to:

- Eliminate what isn't needed
- Sort and organize so that there is logic regarding where and how you store the information
- Consider a layout that is most practical
- Identify a way to stay on top of its organization through maintenance.

Essentially the work to organize digital information follows the same path as physical organization—it just takes less muscle and won't clutter up your room while the project is underway!

Where digital organizing takes a slight variance from organizing "things" is in how you decide to label and store everything. The single line it takes to name a digital file uses the same visual space for a recipe or picture as it does for your doctoral thesis. It's more difficult to scan an area and quickly find what you need. So, setting up files with effective titles and layout is even more vital in the digital world. I tell clients to anticipate what they may be working on or thinking about when they will need to access that document in the future. **Always make retrieval the focus when you decide where and how to file something away.** For example, an emailed receipt could be filed away under "financial," "expenses," "taxes," the calendar year, or myriad other options. The best bet for finding that record again is to ask yourself what you'll be doing when you need that receipt again and then filing it in the most logical place you'd look. Will you need it at tax time? Maybe you'll use it as you pull together expenses for that business trip. Does someone else need access to it? Think in terms of future use (by yourself and others) so that you anticipate where you'd likely go first to retrieve it and set up your categories and files accordingly.

The "sweet spot" for categories of files is to have the fewest necessary to span the breadth of the information being stored yet enough to subdivide and make it easy to find something when you need it. It can be helpful to create a "digital road map" to aid you in deciding on the layout and as a reference later. Start with a blank sheet of paper and capture those records and locations discussed earlier. Then work on drafting the simplest layout to consolidate what you have and design a system that captures it all. If the thought of going back to rework your older file system into the new layout feels overwhelming, you can always start where you are now and simply begin using the new layout going forward. Once things become more familiar and natural, you can choose to go back and move any older records into your new system if you wish. However, it may be perfectly fine to leave earlier files "as is" until they are needed or it's time to purge them permanently.

With the growing ability and trend to move from hard copy to digital information and records, we should discuss a few additional factors that deserve some attention. The first is **passwords**. Love them or hate them, to keep our access and information secure, there needs to be a way to "lock the door" to ensure privacy and safety for our digital footprint. When researching the average number of passwords an individual has, results ranged from 60-100. That's per person! Luckily, many tools are available. Password apps are prevalent and offer high levels of security. An added benefit is accessibility from wherever you are. Tools such as LastPass, NordPass, RoboForm, and those from Norton and Kaspersky are ranked high. Many also offer the ability to generate highly secure new passwords and update your records when those new passwords are created. A quick Google search or visit to the app store can provide a host of options and descriptions. Free versions are often available, but even the paid versions, allowing additional features, are typically very affordable.

If you shy away from using technology for this password storage, you can choose to document by creating a list. Just be sure to acknowledge the value of what that list holds. Give it a designated spot and find a way to keep that information secure—be sure it's somewhere you'll remember! Keeping a backup copy is also wise—try to keep it updated as well and in a location separate from the main list in the event you can't get to one of the copies when needed. Find a secure way, in whatever form you choose, to track those passwords. It's another way to corral your information and minimize the places they're stored. It may also remind you of accounts or access you've forgotten about or may not be top-of-mind.

This last reason leads us to the second factor to consider—**our online presence, information, accounts, and access that exists in the cyber world**. Arranging your online and digital world is important because it is entirely possible that this data will still exist when you leave a job, forget about an infrequently accessed account, replace an old computer, or even pass away. The more you can think through where your online and digital information resides—and how to access it—the easier it will be to avoid your data and accounts staying active or being accessible longer than intended. What digital information have you left behind? Is there any sensitive or private information out there? What work needs to be done to retain or delete that information?

To round out our consideration of the digital "wake" we each leave as we move through life, think about who, other than ourselves, may need access to that information. Granted, the goal is to secure the information so no one can access it but consider what would happen if there were an emergency. Think about your digital presence as a house. Who needs a set of keys? Who would be the person or people you'd call for assistance that may need to tap into your accounts to help during a health crisis, extended travel, or even after your death? That can be an uncomfortable thought, but the work to fully organize not only your physical items but your digital belongings will make things much easier down the road. It's an act of productivity that extends beyond your own reach.

ARRANGEMENT
KEY TAKEAWAYS

Arrangement and organization drive the functionality of a space. Can you find what you need when you need it?

- Are there areas where disorganization causes a loss in your efficiency?
- Are there places where improving organization could boost your productivity?
- Does your workflow work? Does the arrangement of your space best support the activities that happen there?

Identify and address clutter

- Clutter is not only useless items. Even necessary items can be clutter when they accumulate and take over a space.
- Is visual clutter causing a loss of productivity?
- What items are "homeless"? Is there uncertainty about what to *DO* with any of them?

Sorting & Categorization

- Evaluate what's in the space—identify its purpose, what project or person it is linked to, etc.
- What are the main categories of items needed in the space? If unsure, work through what has accumulated. Ask questions. Make items earn their way into your prime area.

Plan your Space with Purpose

- Consider the atmosphere that keeps you productive, ergonomics, layout, workflow, paper management, and your Prime Real Estate.

Storage

- Consider your need for accessibility when selecting *where* to store items.
- Use quality storage items that will hold up to regular use. Consider bins/boxes, file storage, desktop/countertop containers or trays, and labels.

Maintenance

- Even the most organized spaces require maintenance. Build in time to regularly tune up your space.

Purge periodically

- Deciding what to keep—do you need multiples? Has the info been superseded with newer versions? Can you find it elsewhere if you need it?

Online & Digital Organization

- Grow your awareness regarding all the places you keep and store digital records.
- Can you mirror the categories and systems for digital information that you use for physical records, email, or other systems?
- Consider retrieval when filing items away. When will you need to access it? What will simplify the task of locating it when it's needed?
- Establish a secure method for tracking passwords
- Beyond our records and files, remember that our digital presence extends to social media platforms, accounts, etc., in the cyber world. Forethought on accessibility and account closure can be beneficial.

PILLAR 6
RESOURCES

WHAT ARE THE systems or tools that keep you on track? Do you have one place you can reference to provide direction for your day? Or do you rely on your inbox, myriad sticky notes, various lists, or just your memory to hold onto all that needs to get done? What about appointments and other commitments? Perhaps you live and die by your calendar. But what about all the work that needs to happen that isn't tied to a deadline? As life gets busier and your responsibilities increase, how can you juggle it all?

Maybe you are a regular planner—creating prioritized lists and planning your time. Do you refer to your plan regularly, or is it common for you to leave your list at home or forget to look at it throughout the day? Staying on top of all these moving parts is why the use of a planning system is vital. So, do you try that new app everyone is talking about, or would a paper planner be a better choice? Maybe a combination of the two would work best.

So, how do you choose what's right for you? What tool would be best for the job? If you try using a wrench when what you really need is a hammer, the job either won't get done or will take longer than necessary. Select the tools that work best for you and use them to their greatest capability to achieve your highest productivity. Ultimately, the most effective systems are those that fit the user, encompass all the main areas of the user's world, and provide prompts and references that keep you aimed in the right direction at the right time.

This final Pillar—Resources—represents an area of external support regarding your time. It includes those things that keep you running efficiently and smoothly. How do you equip yourself to be productive? **This Pillar addresses the tools that keep you on track and help you monitor progress.**

As we begin to explore the Resources you use, I want to point out how this Pillar differs from the Planning Pillar since both involve the use of a planner, technology, or an app to track time-related activities. When covering Planning, the focus was on the consistent *activity of planning and forethought* regarding your time. Since the tool you use for that purpose is key, this Pillar—Resources—helps you *select the most appropriate and effective mechanism or instrument* to support you as you manage tasks, calendar(s), and reminders.

Planning systems are the focus of this chapter, but we'll also consider the impact other software, workflows, and applications have on your productivity. Are you efficiently using all the tools that are a regular and necessary part of your world? **When the right systems are in place and being maximized, things run more smoothly.**

THE BENEFITS OF A STRONG RESOURCES PILLAR

There's wisdom in recognizing you can't rely solely on your memory to manage ALL you have to navigate, which is where a tailored planning system comes into place—it allows you to work most freely and naturally. It's built around your needs and work style, so there is less chance of things "falling through the cracks." Those strong in this Pillar recognize the value of finding—and using—tools that best support them. Here are some additional ways this area of strength proves beneficial.

You don't sacrifice NOW priorities

Plans can get derailed if we stop to handle something now that truly could wait until a more appropriate time. The tendency is usually rooted in the fear that you'll forget something if it's not dealt with right away. That means priorities take a back seat to interruptions. Those with a robust planning system have the means to capture those items when they arise. Sometimes those interruptions may be deemed urgent, perhaps appropriately so. But for those that truly aren't, having a strong planning system means there's a capture mechanism in place to allow you to put those on hold until a more appropriate time.

You have a reliable system at the ready

A strong planning system helps not only with your weekly and daily planning but also daily management of your attention and priorities. When used consistently, it's the logical "go-to" to capture and reference time-specific appointments and events, tasks, and to-dos, as well as things to plan ahead for upcoming weeks.

You spend less time sampling and implementing new calendars, planners, and lists

Strength in this Pillar reflects a system being in place and running smoothly. As roles, activities, responsibilities, and even work change and grow over time, it is easier to pinpoint where updates should be made. Those with that awareness can more easily target a tool that will work well for them. They spend less time trying new systems, calendars, apps, or checklists in hopes of coming across one that works. They use self-knowledge to make changes and try new things, and there is much less time spent "sampling."

Full efficiency with tools saves time.

The bulk of our focus within this Pillar will be on planning systems, but the theme extends to other systems and tools used regularly. That can mean technology (such as software, applications, and email), paper flow (like file storage, mail processing, and reference docs), and physical tools (for example, supplies, storage, and workspace), which was covered in more detail in the previous section on Arrangement. When you recognize how these systems are key to efficiency, you see the payoff possible when you fully learn and utilize them effectively.

How Does *Your* Resources Pillar Hold Up?

Have you ever stopped to give thought to all the tools that help keep you productive? Many of us don't! Some people simply dive into work, too busy to think about where they could be more efficient in this department. Without any method to stay on track, they may exhibit signs like:

- There is no tool for planning or reference regarding the intended activities/priorities for the days ahead.
- Tasks are done NOW due to a fear they will be forgotten if not done immediately.
- Items get filed away and then forgotten.
- Frequent need to work last minute because something was overlooked until seeing the deadline on the calendar or being reminded by someone.
- Task lists are started—then lost.
- Unfamiliarity with frequently used tools, applications, and systems

The first indicator I explore in this Pillar is the absence of a tool to help track and reference your intended use of time. When I ask clients how they keep track of their activities, most have a calendar, but many lack a consistent method to capture and track those activities they intend to do but don't have a deadline for or aren't scheduled on their calendar. Memory or a basic list may be sufficient when there aren't many things on your agenda or there are only a few areas of oversight to manage simultaneously. However, the more complex your life becomes and the more it draws on your resources of time and energy, the more important it is to find a tool or process to support you.

Another indicator can be the need to stop what you're doing to take care of things when they pop up rather than at an appropriate time. This indicator was mentioned in the last section, as it can also signal difficulty in self-management. Your attention gets caught by things that come up, and it feels like an itch you want to scratch to take care of it NOW. In the context of Resources, it's the absence of a place to capture the activity so that it is flagged for action at a later, more appropriate time. The gap created when an adequate system is not in place means there's nowhere for the action item to be added to the queue, so your instinct tells you, "I better do it now, or I'll forget."

The old saying "Out of sight, out of mind" sometimes applies when it comes to our productivity. When I hear clients say that they forgot about tasks they filed away (intending to return to later) or didn't see approaching due dates or appointments, it prompts me to inquire how and where they note those activities. Maybe time isn't being designated to work on those items that were filed away, or the calendar isn't being referenced far enough in advance to work in anything but a "last minute" mindset. Both situations, as well as the problem of starting and losing multiple lists, merit a look at whether an appropriate planning system is in place and if it is being utilized effectively.

In addition to planning systems, most of us also utilize other tools, applications, platforms, and workflows, whether for work or personal activities. An admission of unfamiliarity or underutilization of those tools warrants further exploration. Investing time in training or practice often saves time in the long run. Many times, it's a simple tip that has made a big impact in using a tool more effectively. This entire Pillar is an acknowledgment that finding the right Resources has value. Considering that experts and professionals rely on top-quality tools and equipment, you should consider the difference between what a basic or generic tool offers versus one tailored to fit you.

MAXIMIZING YOUR TOOLS & RESOURCES
TIPS & TECHNIQUES

A planning system is simply a tool (or bundle of tools) that supports your planning and helps you track your activities, both time-specific and non-time-specific. The search for the perfect planner, calendar, or app is the starting point for many as they take the first steps to improve their productivity. Some will find a single instrument, such as a paper planner or application (Outlook, Google, ToDoist, etc.), can serve all purposes, and others find multiple components most helpful. A means to effectively capture all you need to do and keep track of throughout your day is what most are striving to find. Yet it goes beyond that, as we've covered so far throughout this book.

The tools you use to support you are vital, and finding the best fit absolutely impacts your efficiency. For this reason, this Pillar becomes one of the most tailored and individualized. Personal preferences, work styles, and needs, teamed with all the different jobs, roles, and environments in which we all operate, result in requirements that vary from person to person. That means you're best served when there is deep consideration when selecting that tool. Before we delve into tips and techniques for this Pillar, it's most helpful to step back and consider all the components that go into selecting the system that's right for YOU. Whichever system(s) you choose (we'll cover *how* to choose a system later in this section), you'll want to incorporate the components below. These are what make a planning system robust.

STEP 1
CONSIDER YOUR CALENDAR

Calendars are available in many places and in many forms. In truth, most of us utilize many different calendars for a variety of purposes—some for scheduling, others for tracking. Consider whose schedules most impact your own. Does your job have you using a calendar alongside your colleagues, staff, or department? Do you maintain a family datebook or a child's school planner to track those non-work events? There may also be calendars you use for appointments, bill-paying, volunteer work, etc. These calendars capture information from a variety of sources. To consider what to use for your planning system, determine **which calendar will be your primary tool**. Weigh the following:

- Which one do you reference most frequently?
- Does it need to sync with anyone else's calendar?
- Do you prefer paper or technology?
- Which calendar has adequate space to track everything on your calendar?
- How mobile does it need to be?
- Which calendar can adequately capture all that you need it to contain?

The questions above often lead to the practicality of which calendar is most accessible and workable. Some further considerations are also helpful. Visibility can boost a calendar's usability. Having the option to see a monthly calendar gives a good high-level review of activities coming up, while a daily or weekly view allows more detail and can capture tasks in addition to scheduled appointments and meetings. Many paper planners provide both views, and with technology, the ability to look at the month and drill down to the week or day is a built-in feature. Color coding can also be helpful for some so they can quickly identify entries that are appointments vs. time blocked for work on projects or to identify any number of categories. For instance, visually distinguishing between appointments and project work times means having at-a-glance capability to interpret what's coming up. Plus, it's something easily set up on many technology-based calendars.

Once you've identified your primary calendar, it doesn't require you to eliminate those others you use for specific purposes. Planning is the time when you scan all those calendars for items that will impact your time and must be factored into your schedule, but your primary calendar will be your most inclusive point of reference as you move through your days. During weekly planning, plug in the most relevant events and activities here.

STEP 2
CAPTURE AND MANAGE YOUR TASKS

Where do you track all the stuff you've got to get done? Your calendar tracks those time-specific things, but what about the projects, tasks, and to-dos? Getting a handle on task management is the most common challenge I see in planning systems. Calendars are straightforward and allow specifics—a day and time when the activity is to occur. Tasks, however, can be open-ended, more complex to gather, and harder to track and manage. Some require a single step or action; others involve many moving parts. Some are tied to the calendar through due dates and deliverables. Those tend to get our attention since we see the deadline approaching. But what about tasks that support our life goals? What about the projects that you want to get to "someday"? Some tasks are *now* tasks—others are for *later*. How do you keep tabs on all of them without working from an exhaustive list of ALL your outstanding to-dos? We'll begin by distinguishing between **tasks housed in your capture tools** and your **working task list**.

Think about all the sources that generate your activities and tasks: Where and from whom do you get requests, assignments, and prompts that result in actions you need to take? Who are the people that directly impact your world and your time? An eye-opening exercise is to write down and look at all the places where your tasks are born. The list may contain meetings, emails, calls, or people stopping by your office, clients, friends, various calendars for tracking your or others' schedules, lists, spreadsheets, apps, task and/or project management software, etc. It's surprising to see just how many places funnel tasks and to-dos our way! Is it any wonder it can be tough to effectively manage all of them? Next, you need to gain clarity about how you'll capture those tasks.

Capture Tools

In the earlier Pillar on Planning, we covered the need for the planning process to encompass a 360° view of all the places where tasks may exist. When you fully understand where tasks reside, it reduces the chance that anything will be overlooked. As you review the list created above, some of these represent what I call **capture tools—these are the places that hold the information about things you need to get done, steps you need to take, or goals you want to accomplish.** They may be lists, apps, databases, spreadsheets, etc. Yet we can likely each think of many things we need to do that aren't documented in any official capacity. Tasks can begin or reside in other, less tangible places like post-it notes, ideas that come up during conversations or meetings, text messages, etc. These are the ones that often get overlooked. These are worth thinking about so you can identify a way to catch the action you need to take so you will remember it later. For example, email is not a task list itself, but you may determine that using flags to signify follow-up actions or saving the email to your task list helps you capture work that needs doing. Meetings also often prompt follow-up activities. Where can you capture those next steps and log them for future planning? The result is a thorough look at all the places where tasks are generated and a clear understanding of which capture tool will serve you best so you can revisit them later.

A question may arise as to whether you should only have one capture tool. It's true that having fewer places to look results in simplification and less chance of things being overlooked. What may make the "one tool" option unrealistic is that we capture tasks differently depending on what those items are. For instance, a system you use at work may not be appropriate to house personal tasks. One tool may lend itself to easily tracking large projects, while other lists are more basic and live more naturally in a simple file or document. As you become more intentional with tracking tasks and actively planning, you'll likely find a good balance between sufficient places to capture to-dos and few enough to easily reference them. Whether you end up with one capture tool or use several to span all the areas of your life, the main takeaway is that you have a holding place for all the tasks and to-dos you need to accomplish.

Working Task List

Knowing that you've corralled all your to-dos, projects, goals, assignments, and actions into a central location is a great relief. However, it's still overwhelming to see this all-encompassing and probably very massive list. In truth, it isn't very productive to work from these throughout your days. Efficiency is lost if you need to scan ALL those places to determine what to do next. You may sacrifice some of your prime work time to sorting and making decisions. Additionally, it can be hugely demotivating to work from a long, cumbersome list of tasks and projects. Even on what feels like your most productive days, it's deflating to see only a few items crossed off a miles-long list. The constant reminders and visuals keep your attention divided as you feel the continued weight of undone tasks before you. For this reason, you need to build a bridge between the place(s) where your master task list(s) reside and a more targeted set of intentions for the days ahead. Again, planning serves to span that divide.

During the planning process, you'll distill down those many outstanding tasks into a more manageable list. This working task list should highlight the activities you've prioritized for the week ahead and be realistic, given the time available and the number of scheduled items already on your calendar.

There are different trains of thought on how to be most effective with managing tasks once you've chosen them. For some, the goal is to schedule all activities so that tasks are given a home in your schedule. Plan a specific time to address that activity and get it on your calendar. Another approach is to maintain only appointments and meetings on the calendar while keeping a to-do list separately for those things not tied to a specific time. Between those two approaches is a blend where it proves helpful to schedule work time for some tasks but also pre-select tasks for a given day/week and work from a list as time allows. Finding the right balance is something I work with clients to determine and is dependent largely on the client's work style and preferences. Sampling different approaches can be a good way to find a method that works well for you.

As you consider what your working task list should resemble, make that a key element of your selected planning tool. Adequate space will be needed whether you opt to build tasks into your calendar or via a list.

Incoming information

Your planning system will serve as your road map for direction through the week. It spans the length of time between weekly planning sessions so that you minimize the need to go back and reference all the calendars and task lists in play. But what about all the "stuff" that comes up after you plan? What do you DO with all that new information? Anticipate this as you select your planning system.

When something new comes up—whether it's a note to capture or a task to be done—the first decision is whether it will impact your current plan for the week. If it is an activity, will you schedule it? If it's a task or to-do, when will you plan a time for that work to happen? If it is simply info or a note to be captured, where will you track that? Some capture tools may be readily accessible, and this information can be easily plugged in. For other types of information, you may want to **be sure your planning system allows enough space to jot down items you aren't able to put away in their official capture tool at the moment.** Consider this a "parking lot" to hold these thoughts until you can put them away or schedule them appropriately. When planning comes around next, a look at the new incoming information from the week prior gets added to your review and reset for the week ahead.

So, to recap. Effective systems encompass:

- **Calendars** - Your PRIMARY calendar will be the one you work from; others provide information that can impact your time and factor into your primary calendar.

- **Capture Tools for Projects, Tasks, and To-dos** - These are the holding places for everything you want and need to get done. They may lead up to something on the calendar (like a meeting or deadline), but the work can generally happen at a time to be determined by you

- **Working Task List** - This holds the selected activities for the upcoming days/week. These are chosen from the tasks residing in your various capture tools. You may choose to note them as a specific appointment on your calendar, create a list, or use a blend of those two approaches to work best for you.

- **Sufficient Room for Incoming Information** - If items frequently come up that you may not be able to schedule or file when working throughout the day, determine how much space you'll want to have available for this AND the best way to capture it (paper, electronic, etc.)

STEP 3
SELECT THE RIGHT PLANNING TOOL(S) FOR YOU

Planning systems are highly individualized. Paper planners, calendar-based task lists, and time management applications each have their unique characteristics and speak to various preferences, styles, and needs. Daily tools such as spreadsheets, lists, and workflows can be tailored to the user. Still, other systems may be in place by the decisions of others—company email systems, customer databases, online classrooms, or other software/applications.

It is impossible to outline the broad array of existing productivity, project, and time management tools. Below are some considerations for selecting what type is best for you as well as introducing a few of the most popular and long-standing options.

Paper-Based Tools: Good old-fashioned paper and pen is the option for many. It may lack the connectivity and convenience of some technological solutions, but it shouldn't be discounted entirely. There is a component of writing things down that helps us process information. The tactile work to capture notes via pen or pencil helps some retain and remember information more effectively than typing. This debate has come up in studies involving students who took class notes by hand vs. typing them, with writing coming out on top for retention.

Commonly, even those who rely on technology for much of their system will incorporate some element of paper. Maybe it's just for the quick capture of information that comes in during the day, like "Post-It Notes." Other times it is in that helpful process of getting everything out of your head and jotting down a list of all the thoughts swimming in your mind or documenting some strategy or big-picture thinking. Think about those times that paper proves most effective at organizing your thoughts and ideas.

Paper planners: One of the earliest tools used for time management and productivity is the paper planner, and it continues to be a mainstay for some people today. I am, admittedly, a paper planner person myself. It's simply a statement that this system has proved most helpful to me over the years. I do incorporate some technology into my overall system, but for day-to-day planning and reference, a planner is my go-to tool. With that said, I don't advocate them for everyone. Selecting the right system should incorporate those components outlined earlier, but that's only part of the equation for selecting the tool that can work best for you. Your personal preferences, work styles, and even your environment shape an effective choice.

Paper planner options are available in a variety of styles and layouts and can be found at office supply stores or online retailers. The benefits are that they are typically very straightforward and cost-effective unless you opt to splurge on binders and accessories or for tailored layouts. They are a good visual reference, so keeping them in sight means your plan is near-at-hand. It's also low-risk trying it and realizing you need something different—transitioning to another tool can be done relatively easily.

That said, there are some considerations that may discourage your choice of a paper planner. One of those is portability. Keeping your plan close at hand means you'll need to carry it with you. If you are in one location, that may not be an issue, but if you shuffle between meetings, appointments, or locations throughout the day, is that something you can accommodate? Another is the lack of backup. What happens if you leave your planner behind or lose it? Lastly, you can't plan forward indefinitely. Planners only span a finite stretch of time—planning or booking things well into the future is difficult. None of these need to be a deal-breaker if a paper planner feels like the right solution. Consider if the benefits outweigh those less convenient aspects of this tool.

Worksheets, checklists, and lists: Beyond planners, some everyday paper tools can come in the form of a simple pad of paper, while others are ones we create to fill a specific need. I've seen clients create tailored weekly lists so that they have an outline to prompt them to think about work they intend to do in each area in the coming days. Other documents are born out of necessity to remind us of the steps required. Checklists, forms, and worksheets can simplify work for recurring activities and help walk you through all the needed steps. Even creating a simple weekly or daily "planning page" tailored to your specific needs can be useful when planning. One client used this technique and, each week, printed out a blank template that noted areas for her to consider in her plan: client calls, staff, personal tasks & errands, projects, industry reading, and meeting prep. The tool both guided her thinking as she planned and then served as her task list.

In fact, these tools can be used in paper form OR may be kept online so that they become more technology-based, as we will cover next. Teamed with a calendar, these individualized tools can flesh out a planning system very effectively.

Technology-Based Tools: Here is where the options seem limitless! Technology offers platforms for each planning system component (calendars, task management, and information capturing). Some focus on providing all of these, and others are more singular in the support and capabilities they provide. A small sampling would include the following:

- **Microsoft Office and Google Workspace** Both Microsoft and Google offer a suite of tools that can maximize productivity by using compatible applications.

In addition to the core components of calendars and email, both wrap in communications, presentations, information storage, and other platforms that can streamline our productivity since they address a wide range of needs. In office settings, Outlook is one of the most frequently used platforms, allowing users to view their own calendars alongside other shared calendars for co-workers and teams. The task list component can serve as a capture tool as well as a working task list for the day. Since email can have a huge impact on the way we operate and the flow of information and tasks, having an email component as part of the tool is quite beneficial for some. Similarly, Google offers these capabilities along with its suite of other tools.

- **Project/Task Management software:** Complex activities and projects may benefit from finding the right software. These tools provide tracking, assignment of tasks, organization of information, team access, reporting, and more. They range from basic to fully customizable solutions. Explore not only what these platforms can provide but weigh it alongside your own needs. Do you need the capability to allow multiple users? Does it provide adequate functionality while not being too complex or cumbersome? These options allow you to capture the various steps of projects while helping to drill down to the next, most relevant actions. Some of the most frequently referenced are Asana, Trello, Basecamp, Monday.com, and Todoist, to name a few. A search online for top task management or project management software can turn up a list of those recently reviewed and provide a brief highlight of the capabilities and benefits of each.

- **Information Organization & Beyond:** Going beyond the functionality of email or specific task management are tools such as Evernote which can help organize various types of information. Some of the tools already mentioned above also blend into this category, such as Microsoft Onenote, Google Keep, Todoist, etc. Offering the capability of a web-clipper (catching and storing website pages), online note-taking, and creative design options, you can begin to see the power of how some of these tools can help you save, organize, and retrieve information.

As you look toward these or other technology-based tools, you see how this amplifies the amount of data and information you have at your fingertips. Two of the biggest perks of utilizing technology-based tools are accessibility and portability. Most offer an easy way to retrieve and reference information on the go. Information backups also ensure that the information can't be "lost" in the same way a list or paper document can.

The difficulties some have with technology tools are that they can be complex, and there is a learning curve to become proficient with their use. That learning curve may prove worth the time investment but may feel impossible to someone unfamiliar with a reliance on technology. Another downside is that it can be harder to "work" on the information via technology. The visual prompt to remember a to-do or see a task list is not as obvious when on a small screen. Interacting with information and adding notes can be difficult from a mobile app. Knowing your preferences regarding technology and the likelihood that you will fully utilize and regularly reference technology-based tools is the most helpful consideration when you determine if and how to incorporate these into your planning system.

Schedule Model

In the first section on Planning, we covered the creation of a Schedule Model; this is both an exercise to fit all your important categories and roles into your days and weeks and to draft a general structure for your time to use as a reference. Where this fits in terms of Tools is its use as a resource during planning so that you can build your plan in accordance with the structure and layout you designed.

If you've held space on your schedule model for project work, hobbies, and time with staff or family, what specific task or time will you allot to that space in the week ahead? How can you best note that in your planning system? If your Schedule Model reminds you to align your days with your rhythm and do more focus work in the mornings and meetings in the afternoon, how can you align your schedule to make that happen? Not all weeks can look exactly like your Schedule Model, but that doesn't mean you can't apply it where and when possible. This tool aids planning and can be implemented as you strategize for your week.

Prompts

Next, I encourage you to consider how you best give yourself nudges, cues, and reminders. Chances are, you've relied on various prompts regularly but may not have given them much thought. Effective prompts can redirect our focus when needed and serve as a safety net for those things we might overlook or forget.

A few questions to consider:

- Are you more likely to respond to visual cues, or do auditory alarms serve you best?
- When you need to give yourself a reminder for later, where do you tend to put it? Has that been effective?

- When you file something away, what prompts you to pull it back out when the time is right to address it?

Visual prompts may result in physical clutter if too many items are left out as a reminder to act. Examples are printing out emails and leaving them out where they won't be forgotten, laying an item in our path so that we remember to take it with us or put it away—maybe you leave a stack of books or industry articles in a prime location so that you remember to read them. Strike a balance between using those that serve you well but not so many that disorganization and clutter become an issue.

Alarms can help you track where you are in the day or bring awareness back to an approaching deadline. With technology so readily available, it's easy to set a timer or alarm, making them very handy prompts. You can set an alarm to remind you when it's time to pack up for the day, giving you ample time to get across town for class. They can also signal you've reached the midpoint in your morning and that it's time to gauge where you are in your daily plan. If using them for deeper project work or activities that will require time, make sure you consider where you will be in your day when that notifier goes off. If your prompt doesn't pop up at an opportune time to act, the activity may still be overlooked if you're unable to drop what you're doing and focus on the project at that moment.

Your planning system itself can serve to provide prompts as well. If you can reference your plan and schedule regularly, you may find the number of times you need to rely on a visual cue or alarm is reduced. Your calendar can be utilized for time-specific reminders, decreasing the need for all the physical items in plain view. Your task list can contain a particular action or to-do for an upcoming day when you've set aside time for that category of work. Your planning system proves even more useful when you find ways to build in the prompts that keep you on target.

RESOURCES
KEY TAKEAWAYS

The Resources Pillar is about using appropriate tools to keep you on track and help you monitor progress. They support you in getting done all you need to do.

Planning Systems

- A planning system serves as your dashboard as you move through the week—reflecting your scheduled and non-scheduled activities. Select a tool that fits your preferences (paper, technology-based, or a blend of the two)
- Where are the places tasks are housed or through which to-dos come your way?
- In addition to lists you create, do tasks reside in databases, email, project management software, etc.?
- Maximize your use of existing tools. Are there systems in use in your job, school, or organization that you are not proficient with? Where can you invest in training and get more familiar with those systems so you can operate more effectively?
- Some find success in creating tailored worksheets, checklists, and templates to aid their tracking of activities and tasks.

Schedule Model

- The tool developed during the Planning phase can serve as a tool. When planning, reference the model to see where you can apply that structure to your coming week. Select tasks and activities in support of those categories you worked to incorporate into your schedule.

- Will you need to adjust the schedule model to apply it to the week ahead? If an activity can't happen on Wednesday morning as you prefer, can you shift another time or activity to find time elsewhere?

Prompts

- Determine the best method to provide yourself prompts and reminders. You might employ pop-ups or alarms, but your planning system itself is meant to also be a prompt to keep you on target with your plan.

NOW YOUR WORK BEGINS!

THROUGHOUT THIS BOOK, I've offered up many insights and tips. There is a lot here. It can be an overwhelming number of options, yet it is also just a start. There are many different techniques you can use to reach the same end goal. Apply those that feel like the best fit for you and your needs. Don't be afraid to try new things and work in new ways. You may find that your "best way" is to take an approach offered here and adapt it for yourself. Ideas given within these pages may prove to be thought-starters that help you create your own method. What is *THE* best approach? The one that works for you!

At a higher level, the message I hope you've received throughout this book is that productivity is about more than simply packing more busyness into your day. It's about focusing your attention and actions toward accomplishing what is most important to you. The more I worked with my clients, the more curious I got as to what it is that allows us each to achieve more and feel fulfilled. The 6 Pillars came into focus for me, and I am honored to share it all here with you. Remember that it isn't just about "fixing" areas where you feel like things aren't working. Capitalize on the areas where your skills are sharp. Strengthen those that could provide more support than they currently do. The 6 Pillars each provide unique support to help us be effective. **Good luck on your journey!**

Be sure to connect with Cindy via social media or her website at www.6PillarsProductivity.com for ongoing tips, updates, blogs, and classes.

ACKNOWLEDGEMENTS

SO MANY PEOPLE deserve recognition for the role they played from the time I conceived of this book to its writing and publication. My earliest, constant champion is my husband, Tim, who has encouraged and believed in me every step of the way. To my sons Ethan and Fischer, who are a source of inspiration. And to all my family who has kept tabs on progress and cheered me on.

So many wonderful colleagues and friends also deserve many thanks for their support. To Kim Cox who proofread through some of the earliest versions of these chapters. To my mastermind colleagues Tori Guyer, Kim Oser, Holly Uverity, Lisa Zaslow, and Julie Riber. Having this amazing group of women to help keep me accountable and meet this big goal is priceless. Many others have been part of my professional world and also served to encourage me, allow me space to think out loud, talk about ideas, and listen to the occasional whine of frustration or slacking momentum when my progress felt slower than I'd like. I appreciate each and every one of you!

I also want to acknowledge the team that picked up the reins and helped me move this from original manuscript into a finished product! Diane O'Connell has been a fantastic editor and taught me so much about the craft of authorship. I also want to acknowledge Steve Plummer of SP Designs for his work on the cover and interior design, James King for copyediting and proofreading, and Janet Spencer King for post-production work. I'm so grateful for your expertise and guidance.

Finally, to all my clients over the years. Our work together was the biggest contribution to this book. Thank you for being my teacher while you allowed me to be yours.

APPENDIX
TEMPLATES, FORMS, SAMPLE

Pillar 1: Planning.
Weekly Calendar/Schedule Model Template

	Monday	Tuesday	Wednesday	Thursday	Friday	Saturday
8:00						
9:00						
10:00						
11:00						
12:00						
1:00						
2:00						
3:00						
						Sunday
4:00						
5:00						
6:00						
7:00						
8:00						
9:00						

Appendix: Templates, Forms, Sample

	Monday	**Tuesday**	**Wednesday**	**Thursday**	**Friday**	**Saturday**
8:00						
	Email	Email	Email	Email	Email	
9:00						
		Hold for Client Meetings	Client tasks & projects	**Hold for Client Meetings**	OPEN	
10:00						
	Staff Meeting					
11:00						
12:00						
1:00	Client tasks & projects		OPEN	Marketing Work	**HR tasks/ Team Development**	
2:00						
3:00				**Supervisor Mtg (via Zoom)**		
		Marketing & Prospecting				**Sunday**
4:00						
5:00						
6:00						
7:00						
8:00						

SAMPLE 1 This model was developed by a business owner that has a lot of change and responsiveness within his role and schedule. We held open big spaces for his categories of work to be scheduled.

The 6 Pillars of Productivity

	Monday	Tuesday	Wednesday	Thursday	Friday	Saturday
6:00	Get Ready / Breakfast	Get Ready / Breakfast	Get Ready / Breakfast	Get Ready / Breakfast	Get Ready / Breakfast	Workout
7:00	Networking	Reading??	Complete 1 "Home" Task	Reading??	Networking	"Home" tasks Household paperwork
8:00		8:00 Arrive @ Work		**8:00-9:00 Appt w/ Supervisor**		
	8:30 Arrive @Work		8:30 Arrive @Work		8:30 Arrive @Work	
9:00	PLANNING	9:00-10:30 **Sales Meeting**	9:00-11:30 **Research** *(future projects)*	9:15 Arrive @ Work	OPEN ↓ ↓ Tasks as needed	
10:00	9:30-11:30 **Research** *(future projects)*	**Research** *(current projects)*		9:15-11:30 **Research** *(current projects)*		
11:00						
	Lunch	Lunch	Lunch	Lunch		
12:00		12:30-4:00 **Bookings w/ Clients**		12:30-4:00 **Bookings w/ Clients**	Office Lunch	
1:00	1:00-4:00 **Prospecting** *(cold calls, letters, etc.)*		1:00-4:00 **Prospecting** *(cold calls, letters, etc.)*		1:30 **Invoicing** *(as needed)*	Sunday
2:00					**Admin** *(Desk, Email, Filing, CRM, etc.)*	Church
3:00						Take out trash
4:00						
					Leave Work	
5:00		Leave Work		Leave Work		
	Leave Work	Workout ↓ ↓	Leave Work	Workout ↓ ↓		
6:00						
7:00			Dinner w/Friends			
		"Home" Task		"Home" Task		

SAMPLE 2 This model was for a client who wanted to define a lot of structure and had many pieces he wanted to assign space in his week. He is more in control of his schedule, so he has a lower level of responsiveness that can alter his plan last minute.

Appendix: Templates, Forms, Sample

	Monday	Tuesday	Wednesday	Thursday	Friday	Saturday
8:00	**Tutoring Co-Op**	Clean up & snack prep	Clean up & snack prep	Clean up & snack prep	Clean up & snack prep	
		Focus Time Grading & To-Dos	**Focus Time** Bill Pay	**Focus Time** Grading & Email	**Focus Time** School Planning For next week	
9:00						
		Math	Math	Math	**Flex Day** Activities & Errands	
		Snack & Tutoring (+History Wrap)	Snack & Tutoring Tutoring	Snack & Tutoring (+History Wrap)		
10:00		Recess & Finish morning work	Recess & Finish morning work	Recess & Finish morning work		
		Open Play & Activities	**Open** Play & Activities	**Open** Play & Activities		
11:00						
		11:45 Lunch Prep	11:45 Lunch Prep	11:45 Lunch Prep		
12:00		Lunch	Lunch	Lunch		
1:00		**Down Time**	**Down Time**	**Down Time**		
2:00	**Tutoring Prep for Next Week**	Online Shopping		Menu Planning		
3:00		Snack/Dinner Prep	Snack/Dinner Prep	Snack/Dinner Prep		
						Sunday
4:00	**Swim**					
	Lessons					
5:00		Girl's Night				
6:00				Library		
7:00						

SAMPLE 3 This sample is for a homeschooling parent. We used a blend of more "open days" along with a few very structured days.

The 6 Pillars of Productivity

Monday	Tuesday	Wednesday	Thursday	Friday	Saturday
A.M.	A.M.	A.M.	A.M.	A.M.	
P.M.	P.M.	P.M.	P.M.	P.M.	Sunday
Tasks:	Tasks:	Tasks:	Tasks:	Tasks:	Tasks:

Plan Forward:

Weekly Planning Page Template

Appendix: Templates, Forms, Sample

Pillar 2: Internal Time Clock.
Time Log – Sample 1

Date: _____

Time Started	Task	Time Ended

Time Log – Sample 2

Date: _____

Time	Tasks
8:00 – 9:00	
9:00 – 10:00	
10:00 – 11:00	
11:00 – 12:00	
1200 – 1:00	
1:00 – 2:00	
2:00 – 3:00	
3:00 – 4:00	
4:00 – 5:00	

Time Log – Sample 3

Date: _____

7:30 – 10:00	
10:00 – Lunch	
After Lunch – 2:30	
2:30 – End of Day	
What took MORE time than expected?	
What took LESS time than expected?	

Time Log – Sample 4

Date: _____

Task	I THINK this will take:	How long it Took:

Printed in Great Britain
by Amazon